Believe Us

Believe Us

How Jürgen Klopp transformed
Liverpool into title winners

Melissa Reddy

Harper
North

HarperNorth
111 Piccadilly,
Manchester, M1 2YH

A division of
HarperCollins*Publishers*
1 London Bridge Street
London SE1 9GF

www.harpercollins.co.uk

First published by HarperNorth in 2020

1

The statistics appearing at the front of the book have been compiled courtesy
of Liverpool's official club statisticians Ged Rea and Dave Ball.

A catalogue record for this book
is available from the British Library

HB ISBN: 978-0-00-844195-1
TPB ISBN: 978-0-00-844196-8

Set in Sabon LT Std by Palimpsest Book Production Limited,
Falkirk, Stirlingshire

Printed and bound in Great Britain by
CPI Group (UK) Ltd, Croydon, CR0 4YY

MIX
Paper from
responsible sources
FSC™ C007454

To the family, friends, colleagues and readers who believed in me.

This is a product of your support and encouragement.

Contents

1. Liverpool notched up a 25-point lead at the top of the table this season, the biggest ever gap in English top-flight history.

2. Liverpool achieved 24 consecutive Premier League home wins in the 2019-2020 season, beating Man City's record of 20, achieved between 2011 and 2012.

3. Claiming the title with seven matches to spare, Liverpool bettered Manchester United's earliest title win in 2000/01, and Man City's in 2017/18 – both won the league with five games to spare.

4. With their 1-0 win at Tottenham Hotspur on 11 January 2020, Liverpool set a record of 104 points over 38 consecutive Premier League matches, beating the 102 achieved by Manchester City and Chelsea, ending in 2018 and 2005 respectively. Liverpool extended their record to 110 points from 38 matches (W36 D2 L0) after beating West Ham United 3-2 in February 2020.

5. The 3-1 victory at Brighton & Hove Albion on 8 July was the Reds' 30th this season, and they achieved that mark in a Premier League record of 34 matches.

6. With 61 points from their opening 21 matches, Liverpool won the most points ever accumulated at that stage in any of Europe's top five leagues.

   They went on to extend their record, winning their following six fixtures to rack up 79 points from their first 27 matches, before losing at Watford.

7. Liverpool's 5-3 victory over Chelsea means they joined the Blues, Man Utd and Man City in winning 18 home matches in a Premier League season.

8. With the 3-1 victory in their final match at Newcastle United, Liverpool equalled the 32 victories claimed by Man City in 2017/18 and in 2018/19.

PREMIER LEAGUE RECORDS LIVERPOOL SET OR MATCHED IN 2019-20

1 25-POINT GAP

2 24 CONSECUTIVE WINS

3 EARLIEST TITLE WIN

4 110 POINTS

5 FASTEST TO 30 WINS

6 BEST START EVER

7 MOST HOME WINS IN A SEASON

8 MOST VICTORIES IN A SEASON

JÜRGEN KLOPP'S RECORDS

1. He reached **50** games in charge (in all competitions) in fewer days than any other Liverpool manager in history (217 days).

2. Klopp won **26** of his opening **50** league games — only Kenny Dalglish and Bill Shankly had a better win ratio.

3. He was unbeaten in his first **6** games in all competitions — the longest run without defeat since Bob Paisley and the third longest ever at the helm of Liverpool as a football league club.

4. Liverpool took **48** league games to reach the milestone of **100** goals under the German. It was achieved in the joint fewest number of top-flight matches, shared with Kenny Dalglish in 1986.

5. Klopp's first goalscorer as a Reds manager was also a German — Emre Can against Rubin Kazan in the Europa League in October 2015.

6. He became the first Liverpool manager in history ever to win his first **3** derby matches in charge.

7. His team took **197** games to record **400** goals — faster than any other Reds boss.

JÜRGEN KLOPP'S RECORDS

8. Liverpool accumulated **300** league points in **146** games — the fewest games required by any Reds boss to reach the landmark.

9. Klopp oversaw more victories (**92**) in his first **150** league games in charge than any other Liverpool manager in history.

10. In 2019 he became the **5th** German coach to win the European Cup/Champions League after Dettmar Cramer, Jupp Heynckes, Ottmar Hitzfeld and Udo Lattek

11. He was the **1st** manager ever to take an English team to three European finals in his first three seasons of European competition.

12. Games Liverpool came from behind to win under Klopp (all competitions):

    2015-16   6 of 22 (27%)

    2016-17   5 of 11 (45%)

    2017-18   3 of 14 (21%)

    2018-19   5 of 8 (63%)

    2019-20   6 of 11 (55%)

I

A Club Divided

'We are still in the process of reversing the errors of previous regimes. It will not happen overnight.'
John W Henry

Football was no longer enjoyable, no longer an escape. Liverpool Football Club were once 'the greatest team the world has ever seen', but they hadn't been for a while. For 25 years, the club watched as others — chiefly Manchester United — displaced them as the cream of England. The obsessive desire to win the league increasingly began to wear on players and staff, while disillusionment enveloped the fanbase. Near misses were followed by complete fall offs. There were triumphs in cup competitions and moments to eternally savour, but it was never enough. By September 2015, according to one long-serving employee at their Melwood training facility, Liverpool had been reduced to a 'bunch of parts that didn't feel like they belonged together. It was a miserable place to be. You knew the fans were fed up, you knew the players were drowning and there was bickering among the coaching staff. Nothing felt right'.

Liverpool had entered the month on the back of a demoralising 3–0 defeat by West Ham at Anfield, closely followed by a meek surrender and 3–1 defeat at Old Trafford to Manchester United. When manager Brendan Rodgers was quizzed about what was needed to change the team's fortunes, his words were empty football-speak — 'we need to want the ball more, we need to train harder' — heightening the concerns of Liverpool's owners.

Fenway Sports Group feared the stench of the 2014–15 season, which featured an abysmal non-performance in an FA Cup semi-final exit at the hands of Aston Villa and ended with a 6–1 humiliation at Stoke City, would linger well into the new campaign. They circled the October international break as the perfect window to shred the script and start afresh. With the exception of the Merseyside derby at Goodison Park, which was the final fixture before the hiatus, there was a list of very winnable games coming up — with four at home — for Rodgers to earn a stay of execution.

But Liverpool stumbled to a 1–1 draw at Bordeaux in the Europa League, before the same result at Anfield against Norwich City in the top flight later that week.

Lowly Carlisle United came to Merseyside in the League Cup third round, with the hosts only scraping through on penalties after a torrid display. Toxicity filled the terraces at Anfield and it showed no signs of dissipating, especially not with supporters witnessing an unconvincing 3–2 win at home over Aston Villa, before yet another 1–1 draw in Europe, this time against little-known FC Sion.

While events on the pitch could be filed under certified disasters, soundtracked by boos from the Kop, decisive action was being taken in the boardroom. Liverpool's chief executive at the time, Ian Ayre, made a call in mid-September that would alter the course of Liverpool's history. He dialled Marc Kosicke, the agent of Jürgen Klopp, which led to a Skype call between the men. A face-to-face meeting between the German, who was on holiday having resigned from Borussia Dortmund four months earlier, and Liverpool's hierarchy was pencilled in for 1 October 2015 in New York — the day of the club's lethargic showing against FC Sion. But more on that later.

At Melwood, it was hard to escape the growing sense that Brendan Rodgers was on borrowed time. For some, it was surprise that the Northern Irishman was still in the job after the horror show at Stoke, which coincided with Steven Gerrard's farewell game for Liverpool. Managers rarely climb out of the debris of such abominations unscathed, especially when large swathes of that 2014–15 season were best forgotten.

Supporters, too, were shocked. As Neil Atkinson, host of the award-winning fan media collective *The Anfield Wrap* wrote, 'If Rodgers wasn't a man fighting with himself at the start of 2014–15, he most definitely was by the end — and the thing about fighting with yourself is that you will always lose.

'Liverpool lost. They lost and lost and lost. And then Stoke. Stoke was the final straw – how can you trust the man who oversees losing 6–1? For those who were there, Stoke would live long in the memory. What do you do about that? How do you rebuild those bridges? To have kept him beyond that point now feels tougher on him than on us.'

Deciding whether to stick or twist after the calamity at the Britannia Stadium was not straightforward. The owners had anticipated teething problems after the exhilarating but failed title tilt of 2013–14, which was followed by Luis Suarez's departure to Barcelona. Despite the many controversies that surrounded him, Suarez had been the reference point and the fuel for Liverpool's ambitions, and as Rodgers later reflected 'the whole thing exploded' when the Uruguayan moved on.

Having blocked his move to Arsenal the previous summer, Liverpool knew Suarez would exit in 2014 and pre-empted it by tying him to a new contract with a higher release clause of £75 million. It was still a snip for a player of his gifts, but Barça snapped him up for £10 million less than that fee after he was suspended from all football-related activity for four months for biting Italy defender Giorgio Chiellini during the World Cup.

Liverpool had a long time to prepare for life without their talisman but botched it. A process that started with priority target Alexis Sanchez joining Manchester United instead, was followed by next choice Loïc Rémy from Chelsea failing a medical, before the final pick was between an aged Samuel Eto'o and Mario Balotelli. Rodgers had publicly said he 'categorically' didn't want the latter, but the maverick Italian was the player he got.

Balotelli was one of eight new first-team signings bought to the tune of £107.5 million to cushion the blow of losing Suarez. It was neither the wisest approach nor the best use of the money given to the manager, and other members of Liverpool's transfer committee were, as one senior staffer put it, 'not in the same book let alone on the same page' in designing the squad.

With so many incomings, FSG understood there would be a reset of sorts. Adam Lallana was part of that mass recruitment drive during the summer transfer window of 2014, the midfielder costing £25 million from Southampton. He recalls how arduous his debut season was. 'There were so many new players signed:

a lot of different cultures, characters, languages and playing styles all coming together,' says Lallana, who would go on to spend six years at Anfield before joining Brighton in July 2020.

'It was a big adjustment for us, but also for the guys already at the club. We needed time to settle, but the expectation was huge. Liverpool lost Suarez, and Sturridge was injured, so the goals were effectively taken out of the team, yet there was still this pressure to go one better and win the league. It was a really difficult place to be in 2014–15 and things felt disjointed.

'The way the season ended with that 6–1 defeat at Stoke City was really demoralising. We then lost Stevie [Gerrard] and Raheem [Sterling]. It only increased the pressure. It was intense. There was more fear than freedom and not a lot of confidence around.'

When FSG sat down with Rodgers to deconstruct such a pitiful season, they had underscored that it wasn't just the listless performances that were a problem, but the anxious atmosphere around the club and lack of direction. While the owners appreciated the mitigating circumstances — reconfiguring the team post-Suarez, injuries, new signings needing to settle — they believed the manager hadn't extracted the best from the squad. He was also underplaying his own hand by not fully integrating, trusting and maximising the strengths of those players he didn't particularly want at the club.

FSG felt there weren't enough ideas and diverse viewpoints being encouraged, with the manager's coaching staff essentially only facilitating his plan rather than highlighting holes or offering suggestions.

There was an acceptance from Rodgers that a freshening up of the backroom team was needed to address the problems. His long-serving assistant Colin Pascoe was sacked and the contract of first-team coach Mike Marsh wasn't renewed. Both decisions proved universally unpopular at the training complex, with players and staff outspoken about their views. Worse still, was the selection of Sean O'Driscoll as the new assistant manager.

'When those changes happened, the dynamic completed shifted,' says one employee who works closely with the backroom team. 'It really didn't sit well with anyone. Sean had a totally different opinion to Brendan and would openly counter his philosophy in a very abrupt way. He would say, "Why do we need to build from the back when we don't have the players for it? Just smash it long." He would go against the manager's ideology and it would make the staff very uncomfortable as we had to argue with him.

'We needed to all be pulling in the same direction, we needed consistency, we needed repetition, we needed to be convinced of our plan, but we didn't have that. Sean rubbed a lot of people up the wrong way. His mannerisms, his personality, his way of speaking to people wasn't what we were used to. Everything was different, everything was up in the air and didn't feel right.'

Former Liverpool player Gary McAllister was also added to the set-up as first-team coach, with Dutchman Pep Lijnders promoted from the academy to become first-team development coach.

'There was probably too much that was new, too much to figure out during a pre-season when we just had to hit the ground running,' the employee continues. 'Dealing with Sean was the biggest thing to get used to. It was apparent that it wasn't going to work and it was apparent that it wasn't going to work very quickly.'

During that summer, FSG still hoped Rodgers and his coaching staff could navigate Liverpool back to the right path. They had to back him. Jürgen Klopp, their ideal choice as a replacement, wanted to recharge his batteries 'after seven intense and emotional years' at Borussia Dortmund, and was going to 'take a break until further notice'.

For all the unease from the owners over how far away Liverpool were travelling from their expected direction, it was offset by the residual joy of the 2013–14 campaign, where the club missed out on the Premier League title by just two points while scoring 101 goals. And for all his faults as a young manager,

Rodgers was a skilled tactician and excellent on the training pitches. Despite muddling through 2014–15, he was still the reigning League Managers Association Manager of the Year. Talents like Luis Suarez, Daniel Sturridge, Raheem Sterling and Philippe Coutinho had elevated their play under his guidance, with tweaks helping them find the edge to become a feared creative and attacking foursome on the pitch.

'He helped me with my runs, arriving in the area at the right time and coming in from wide, which benefited my confidence,' Suarez would explain two years after leaving Anfield. 'We worked hard on finding ways I could isolate players and then try to beat them, man on man. That was the only way I could succeed in England . . . I wasn't proven and I had to adapt to the Premier League, which Brendan knew. He knows all about English football and he educated me to become successful.'

When Manchester City paid Liverpool £49 million for Sterling in July 2015 — then a record sum for an English player — it was largely on account of the positional and tactical dexterity the forward had learnt while working with Rodgers.

When Brendan Rodgers parted company with Swansea City to become manager of Liverpool in June 2012, his panoramic view of the game, carved from travelling around Europe for an in-depth education from different leagues, clubs and managerial minds, was welcomed. He could communicate with players in multiple languages and was very popular with the ones he didn't ostracise at Liverpool.

While Rodgers had a painful habit of falling into superficiality and unnecessarily selling himself at every opportunity, most at the club remember him as a warm man, who had a tireless work ethic. His upbringing on a council estate in County Antrim's Carnlough — where he was taught the value of creating a living by his dad, Malachy, and the importance of empathy by his mum, Christina — underpinned everything he did. Rodgers sadly lost both his parents early: his mother, who volunteered for an Irish charity, was 52 when she had a sudden heart attack. Not long after, his father succumbed to throat cancer aged 59.

Family was a powerful element for Rodgers and he often tried to motivate the squad by plugging into their loved ones. In his autobiography, *Crossing The Line*, Luis Suarez revealed the special touch Rodgers applied to pre-match team talks as they chased the title in 2013–14. 'He had contacted our mothers, one by one, and asked them to write something about their sons,' the forward explained. 'Before every game, as we went on the run which saw us come so close to winning the title, he would spend the final few minutes before we went out reading what one of them had said in front of the whole team. The final word came not from the manager, but a player's mum.'

In early 2014, Rodgers had learnt that a club employee based at Liverpool's city centre offices in Chapel Street was due to undergo a kidney transplant. The night before surgery, the manager called to wish him the best, encouraging the patient to focus on the betterment of his life after the procedure. It had an uplifting effect that hasn't been forgotten.

When Raheem Sterling was continuously transgressing off the pitch in his teenage years, Rodgers helped him steer away from trouble and towards making the game his life. 'He helps me a lot with not just my football but if I need someone to talk to about off the field then he's there for me,' the England international would admit. 'He's helped me massively, especially on the pitch as well, so I have to give credit to him and thank him a lot.'

As Christmas neared in 2013, Jordan Henderson's father, Brian, was diagnosed with throat cancer. When the former policeman eventually shared the devastating news with his son, the midfielder leaned on Rodgers for support. The manager himself had been through the turmoil of learning his dad had the same illness and could relate to the struggle of trying to balance personal torment with excelling professionally.

Henderson was granted extra time off by Rodgers while Brian went through successful treatment to remove lymph nodes from both sides of his neck and a tumour from his tongue.

Rodgers was a rock and encouraged the England international to leave everything out on the pitch for his father. In the next four out of five fixtures Henderson played, he was man of the match. That period still lingers in the player's memory and is perhaps partly why there was a great sense of guilt when Rodgers was ultimately relieved of his duties at Liverpool on 4 October 2015 following a 1–1 away draw with Everton.

'When Brendan left, as a player you feel a responsibility that we all haven't done our jobs properly and someone loses theirs because of it – someone who I thought was a very good coach and a very good manager,' Henderson says. 'And when someone loses their job, it's really not a nice feeling, it's horrible. When Brendan got sacked, it was difficult news to take. I personally believed I should have done more on the pitch to help him.'

In truth, there was no reason for Henderson to feel that way. The relationship between Liverpool's owners and Rodgers was doomed from the outset as it was founded on an unhappy compromise in 2012 that neither wanted.

After bringing to an end club legend Kenny Dalglish's second spell as Liverpool manager, FSG wanted to fully revolutionise the club. Intent on following the European model, they were keen to hire a director of football to oversee operations, including transfers, in order to holistically shape the club moving forward.

At the time, FSG made loose enquires to ascertain whether Jürgen Klopp could be prised from Borussia Dortmund, but the answer was emphatically negative. Rodgers emerged as their first-choice option, but he favoured the old-school, autocratic route of managers being in sole control. He refused to accept the job if a director of football position was established.

What followed was a patchwork of both preferences, that made little sense as neither party fully bought into it. On 31 May 2012, Liverpool's official statement on the appointment declared: 'Rodgers' primary focus will be the first team but he'll also work extensively in collaboration with the new football operations structure as the team adheres to the continental football Sporting Director mode.'

However, at his first opportunity to speak on the matter, their new managerial recruit was quick to state, 'One of the things you need to do is to know yourself, and I know myself. I know what makes me work well and that wouldn't have been a model I would have succeeded in. It's absolute madness if you are the manager of the club and someone else tells you to have that player. It doesn't work.' Already, the men in the boardroom and the man in the dugout were at odds over a crucial point: how to actually run the operation.

What Liverpool settled on was 'a collaborative group of people working to help Brendan deliver the football side of it,' as Ayre termed it.

The transfer committee was born with the correct idea, but under the wrong circumstances and leadership. The chief executive was part of the brains trust, which also featured Michael Edwards (then the director of technical performance), head of recruitment Dave Fallows and Barry Hunter, the chief scout. Rodgers was a key component of the committee and had 'the final say' on all incomings and outgoings at Liverpool, but to his chagrin, the decision-making process was collaborative.

'I wanted to make sure that I would be in charge of football matters; that I would control the team,' Rodgers said at the time. What he failed to understand was that he could do that while accepting the suggestions from some very sharp minds and a leading analytical research team on how to build a balanced squad for the long-term.

From the off, there were issues. During the first summer window under Rodgers in 2012, Liverpool were on the verge of signing Daniel Sturridge from

Chelsea only for the manager to tank the deal because he wanted Clint Dempsey from Fulham instead and was willing to offer Henderson in part-exchange. The club had already offloaded Andy Carroll to West Ham on loan and FSG emphasised the need to bring in a striker to fortify the attack, but their advice was ignored.

Rodgers went all in on the USA international, whose valuation of £7 million at the time did not tally for a player in his late twenties entering the final year of his contract. The owners did not want to sanction a deal for Dempsey that screamed of short-termism and they were privately annoyed that the transfer of Sturridge, who would eventually switch to Anfield in January 2013, was derailed.

What really incensed them, however, was when Rodgers told the press that letting Andy Carroll go was 'probably 99.9 per cent finance. If we've got a choice, then he's someone around the place who you could use from time to time. He would have been a good option'. Rodgers would later contradict himself by stating he had the courage to get shot of the Geordie, who was Liverpool's record signing at the time, because he didn't fit the club's ethos. He went further still when that window closed to fuel talk that he wasn't being financially backed by FSG.

'I was very confident I had a deal sewn up, but it has gone and I can't do anything about it,' he said on the negotiations for Dempsey, who joined Tottenham instead. 'There's no point me crying about it or wishing we had or hadn't done this or that.'

Those public declarations drove John W Henry, the Boston Red Sox and Liverpool principal owner, to pen an open letter to the club's fans explaining their methodology. 'The transfer policy was not about cutting costs,' he wrote. 'It was — and will be in the future — about getting maximum value for what is spent so that we can build quality and depth.

'We are still in the process of reversing the errors of previous regimes. It will not happen overnight. It has been compounded by our own mistakes in a difficult first two years of ownership. It has been a harsh education, but make no mistake, the club is healthier today than when we took over.

'Spending is not merely about buying talent. We will invest to succeed. But we will not mortgage the future with risky spending. After almost two years at Anfield, we are close to having the system we need in place. The transfer window may not have been perfect but we are not just looking at the next 16 weeks until we can buy again; we are looking at the next 16 years and beyond. These are the first steps in restoring one of the world's great clubs to its proper status.

'It will not be easy, it will not be perfect, but there is a clear vision at work. We will build and grow from within, buy prudently and cleverly and never again waste resources on inflated transfer fees and unrealistic wages. We have no fear of spending and competing with the very best but we will not overpay for players.

'We will never place this club in the precarious position that we found it in when we took over at Anfield. This club should never again run up debts that threaten its existence.'

Henry's words resonate now, but they didn't throughout Rodgers' tenure, because there was a dual policy at play, which led to dysfunction on the pitch. Edwards, Fallows and Hunter would get their preferred targets like Emre Can from Bayer Leverkusen and Hoffenheim's Roberto Firmino, while the manager was able to bring in his own targets with the likes of Joe Allen and Christian Benteke.

The purchase of Allen from Swansea City was another divisive episode. Liverpool were dithering over meeting the £15 million valuation for the Wales international and Rodgers, still early into the job, threatened to resign if the deal didn't get over the line.

The hierarchy hoped this was a case of the committee finding their feet and learning how to find common ground. That was unfounded. Rodgers' signing of Benteke from Aston Villa for £32.5 million in July 2015 — his last deal for the club — spotlighted just how fudged the strategy was. Earlier that month, Liverpool were celebrating beating rivals to the £29 million capture of Firmino, believing him to be the club's long-term No 9. Yet they then spent even more money on a target man that stylistically contrasted with the team in order to appease the manager.

It couldn't continue. When Rodgers first met FSG over the Liverpool job, he had produced an impressive 180-page dossier titled 'One Club, One Vision', but there was no unified approach during his tenure.

Henry was right. Liverpool were 'close to having the system we need in place', but it required an elite figure to completely believe in it and to galvanise it. Fortunately, they knew just the man for that.

2

The Perfect Fit

'From tomorrow I will be the Liverpool man 24/7.'

Jürgen Klopp

'We're hitting for the cycle,' John W Henry smiled to FSG chairman Tom Werner and its president Mike Gordon. In baseball, the terminology refers to the achievement of one batter recording a single, double and triple hit as well as a home run in the same game. It is uncommon and one of the most difficult feats to accomplish in the sport.

As the trio took in the East Manhattan skyline from a 50-storey skyscraper housing the offices of law firm Shearman & Sterling on Lexington Avenue, they were primed to swing big in a meeting they believed had the power to reshape not just Liverpool FC but the football landscape.

Henry was equating being on the cusp of hiring the perfect manager for the club — an incredibly complex criteria to meet — to hitting for the cycle. No fanbase deifies the main man in the dugout as vociferously as Liverpool's: through banners, in song and the manner in which they are tattooed to the very soul of the institution. It's a phenomenon that stretches back to Bill Shankly's appointment in 1959, with the Scot transforming a club in the Second Division into a 'bastion of invincibility' during his 15-year dynasty.

Equally, no fanbase are as demanding of what they want in their leader. At Anfield, the requirements stretch well beyond what a CV reads or being tactically excellent. You need to win, connect with supporters and represent the essence of Liverpool on a cultural, political and spiritual level. In summary, a top manager must also operate as a man of the people while illustrating he is bigger than the job, greater than the expectations and unwavering in his handling of the fiercest criticism.

In New York on 1 October 2015, FSG were confident they were going to hire that very figure. A magnetic individual who had the proven capacity to galvanise, rejuvenate and deliver sustainable success to a club, while also having a lasting impact on the place and its populace.

'It's the right guy at the right time,' Gordon noted.

But the owners had selected the wrong choice of day for their first face-to-face interaction with Jürgen Klopp. The meeting coincided with the annual gathering of the United Nations general assembly, which gridlocked New York. The German's journey from JFK Airport to Lexington Avenue took six hours in snaking traffic, and while it was unwelcome, it didn't diminish his 'highest enthusiasm' for the opportunity to outline his vision for Liverpool.

Long before Klopp stepped into the building, the job was his. It was not an interview, rather a confirmation of what FSG already knew about the two-time Bundesliga winner courtesy of a call, a Skype conversation, and crucially, a detailed 60-page dossier on his way of working. Compiled by Liverpool's esteemed head of research, Ian Graham, and Michael Edwards, who was technical director at the time, it evaluated everything from the manager's training sessions, reaction to setbacks, achievements in relation to his resources as well as his interaction with staff and players through first-hand testimony from his former clubs Mainz and Borussia Dortmund. The more Liverpool drilled into Klopp's methodology, the greater their conviction was that he could unify the core areas of the club and elevate it.

Beyond the comprehensive document, FSG knew he was their guy because they had previously pursued him twice. Each time they sought a manager, he stood out and tallied with their long-term thinking. Towards the end of 2010, as Roy Hodgson was scraping through a painful spell at Liverpool's helm that would eventually span only 31 games in charge, the group used a third party to ascertain whether Klopp would consider leaving Dortmund to move to Anfield. It was no surprise the answer was negative, given he was successfully re-establishing BVB as a Bundesliga and European force while they played irresistible, high-pressing football.

A year later, another tentative approach was made when club legend Kenny Dalglish, Hodgson's replacement, was released from his second stint at Liverpool. 'I have been made aware of interest in England, and it is an honour to be linked with big clubs in the Premier League,' Klopp said, before emphasising, 'I love it here [at Dortmund] and have no intention of changing clubs.'

Naturally, Liverpool were not the only English team trying to secure the elite manager, who had halted, at least temporarily, Bayern Munich's monopoly on being Germany's best. Winning back-to-back Bundesliga titles and bulldozing opponents in the Champions League, where Dortmund reached the final in 2013, meant that interest in Klopp ballooned — especially 30 miles away in Manchester. While Dalglish's successor as Liverpool manager, Brendan Rodgers, was overseeing poetry in motion on Merseyside in early 2014 with a Luis Suarez-powered offensive line taking the club close to the title, David Moyes was horribly floundering at Manchester United. Sir Alex Ferguson's successor was well out of his depth and urgent action was necessary to remedy the club's demise. Their executive vice-chairman, Ed Woodward, scheduled a chat with Klopp in Germany to sell him on making the switch to Old Trafford.

The BVB trainer hugely admired Ferguson's achievements and the manner he went about establishing United as a global juggernaut, which is largely why he agreed to the encounter. Woodward's pitch, however, was the antithesis of what would appeal to Klopp. He spotlighted their financial might and offered an Americanised picture of blockbuster names and entertainment while likening United and Old Trafford to the game's Disneyland.

Klopp, a football romantic who feeds off emotion and who counts time spent on the training pitches as more fundamental than transfers, was turned off.

That came as no shock to Christian Heidel, the former sporting director of Mainz. He has a three-decade relationship with Klopp and was the one who offered him the chance to instantly progress from being a player to the club's manager. 'Emotionally powered' is one of the core descriptors he uses for his friend, who is also a 'fighter' and 'builder'. Heidel knew Klopp's powers could only be properly unleashed at places that resonate with his own personal experiences. Being at United and having an unlimited budget would jar with a life shaped by scaling adversity and making the most out of little.

Klopp's formative years in Glatten, a tiny but picturesque town in the Black Forest, were simple. His late father, Norbert, who had been a promising goalkeeper and earned a trial at Kaiserslautern as a teenager, worked as a salesman specialising in dowels and wall fixings. He was a ruthless competitor, extracting the maximum from his son by never taking it easy on him, whether it came to skiing, tennis, football or sprints across the field. Norbert impressed on him that it wasn't worth doing anything without full dedication. He taught his son that 'attitude was always more important than talent', promoted a ferocious work ethic and schooled him in the art of resilience.

Klopp junior, a Stuttgart fan, had an unsuccessful trial with his boyhood club and did not become a professional footballer until he was 23. In the interim, he turned out for Pforzheim, Eintracht Frankfurt II, Viktoria Sindlingen and Rot-Weiss Frankfurt while working part-time in a video rental store and loading lorries. He juggled that with taking care of his toddler, Marc, while also studying for a degree in sports business at Goethe University Frankfurt.

'Life took me a few places and gave me a few jobs,' Klopp noted. 'It wasn't about where I could be, but about doing what I had to do, because I was a young father and needed to provide.' After finally landing a pro contract with Mainz in 1989 as an industrious but technically-limited striker, Klopp still took steps to invest in his future for the benefit of his family. Earning just £900 a month, he signed up to the legendary Erich Rutemöller's coaching school in Cologne. Twice a week, he would undertake the 250-mile round trip to enhance his tactical understanding of the game.

Klopp also sponged off Wolfgang Frank, the late Mainz coach who was inspired by Arrigo Sacchi's Milan. He would spend hours talking to him about systems and the secrets to overpowering better resourced opponents. 'Under Wolfgang Frank, for the first time in my career, I had the feeling that a coach has a huge impact on the game,' Klopp would reveal. 'He made us aware that a football team is much more independent of the class of individual players than we thought at the time. We have seen through him that it can make life very difficult for the opponent through a better common idea.'

Frank was one of the first German managers of the era to shun using a sweeper, which was the norm, opting for a four-man zonal defence and a midfield diamond shape. He espoused high-pressing, attacking from inside, offensive protection and overloading the flanks — all hallmarks of Klopp's teams to the present-day Liverpool.

Those tactics became the blueprint for Mainz in February 2001 when manager Eckhard Krautzun was sacked by the club on the eve of an away game and sporting director Christian Heidel called an emergency summit with senior players. It was decided at the meeting that Klopp, who had been converted to a defender from a striker, would undergo another transformation and become their new manager. The choice was unanimous and as with his playing career, the need to defy convention and recover from setbacks would be the driving force in his new managerial setup.

Klopp is unrivalled in dealing with massive disappointments and moulding them into both lessons and motivation. 'Even when you don't want defeats, when you have it, it is very important to deal with it in the right way,' he said on looking back at his career in the game. 'I had to learn that early in my life, especially my coaching life. We had so many close failures: like with Mainz not going up by a point, not going up on goal difference, then getting up with the worst points tally ever; Dortmund not qualifying for Europe, then losing a Champions League final. I am a good example that life goes on. I would have had plenty of reasons for getting upset and saying, "I don't try anymore."

'Obviously, it is not easy to go through these moments, but it is easier to deal with it because it is only information, and if you use it right the feeling is good.'

That is pure Klopp. And it was why Hans-Joachim Watzke, Dortmund's CEO, was convinced he would reject United's offer. Their money-based pitch clashed with rather than complemented the manager's make-up. In the second week of April 2014, Klopp told Watzke he'd be swerving the chance to take charge at Old Trafford. As he once summarised: 'You can be the best in the world as a coach, but if you are in the wrong club at the wrong moment, you simply don't have a chance.'

Enquiries from Manchester City and Tottenham would both also be rebuffed a few months later. A year after shunning United, however, Klopp's circumstances at Signal Iduna Park changed considerably.

With Dortmund regularly ceding their greatest talents to European football's apex predators — chiefly Bayern — they found that continuing to usurp their powered-up rivals in the Bundesliga was becoming too taxing. BVB's results were no longer as good as their performances, with staleness and a sense of comfort creeping in. During a press conference that reverberated around the world on 15 April 2015, Klopp announced he would be leaving Dortmund at the end of the season. At the time, the club were 10th, 37 points behind Bayern. The city in Germany's North Rhine-Westphalia was enveloped in sadness.

'I always said in that moment where I believe I am not the perfect coach anymore for this extraordinary club I will say so,' Klopp stated. 'I really think the decision is the right one. I chose this time to announce it because in the last few years some player decisions were made late and there was no time to react.'

Fast forward five months and the atmosphere couldn't have been more of a contrast in an expansive boardroom at the New York offices of Shearman & Sterling, where over the course of four hours, Klopp sketched his plan to restore Liverpool as a global and continental powerhouse.

He addressed the lack of an on-pitch identity, which would be the first facet to rectify, and also pointed out the importance of harnessing the emotional pull of the fans. From the academy through to the first-team operation at Melwood, Klopp outlined a blueprint for the club's playing style and standards to be aligned. For Liverpool to have any chance of becoming a force again, he reasoned, they would have to operate as one formidable unit.

Mike Gordon remembers being 'in awe' of Klopp, not on account of his magnetic personality, but the substance of his strategy and the concise yet convincing way he delivered it in a second language.

It is why, just an hour into spelling out his vision, FSG told Klopp's agent, Marc Kosicke, that their lawyers had begun drafting his contract of employment. When the juncture came to discuss personal terms at the end of the talk, the manager excused himself and took a walk through Central Park. As Klopp stood soaking in the sights of the Hallett Nature Sanctuary, it dawned on him that it was not the type of surveying he had originally contemplated after his break from football.

As a player, he was fascinated by watching how managers work — from implementing their philosophies to handling different personalities, balancing squad dynamics and drafting plans that extended beyond match preparation. Klopp had resolved to travel around Europe to absorb as much knowledge as possible from coaches when he hung up his boots. However, his immediate transition from pulling on a shirt for Mainz to becoming their manager paused that idea for seven years. Switching from the Opel Arena to Dortmund further shelved it for the same amount of time and now Klopp was fresh off a four-month sabbatical and about to become Liverpool manager.

That night, when he returned to his suite at the Plaza Hotel, he thought about how he wouldn't change anything about his path, his choices or the timing of them, relating as much to his wife, Ulla Sandrock.

That same evening, Liverpool stumbled to yet another dispiriting draw at Anfield. The sound of the final whistle against FC Sion was met with booing for the third time in four games at the famed ground. Over in the Bronx, the Red Sox were defeated 4–1 by the Yankees, their greatest rivals. Yet those results couldn't dilute FSG's celebratory mood after finally securing the manager they had coveted since their takeover of Liverpool in 2010.

Back at Melwood, it was hard to escape the feeling that Brendan Rodgers' time was running out. After Liverpool's 1–1 draw at Goodison Park on 4 October that left them 10th in the league table, Rodgers was driving back home, when he received a phone call from Mike Gordon relieving him of his duties. News of his departure quickly broke, with Klopp's status as the prime candidate to replace the Northern Irishman dominating the coverage.

Conversations at Liverpool's training complex centred around him being so heavily linked with the job. 'There was such a buzz and he was really high profile as well, which got the lads going,' Adam Lallana recalls. 'I remember us sitting in the canteen discussing that he ticks all the boxes for Liverpool. We weren't going to outspend the likes of City, United and Chelsea and he wasn't a big-money manager. He had a history of improving clubs by making the players he had better before building on that base. We spoke about games we'd seen of Dortmund, about things we'd read or heard about the gaffer and there was so much excitement around the place.'

Jordan Henderson was at the Bernabeu in April 2013 to watch BVB line up against Real Madrid in the second leg of their Champions League semi-final. Dortmund took a 4–1 advantage to Spain and lost 2–0 after late goals from Karim Benzema and Sergio Ramos, but still progressed to the climax of the competition at Wembley.

'I was fortunate enough to go watch Dortmund against Madrid at the Bernabeu and I was really blown away by how clear their identity as a team was and how they controlled large parts of such an important game against a side with superior resources,' Henderson says. 'They lost the match, but it didn't matter because they managed the tie well and you expect to be put under pressure by Real, especially when they're at home and need to win, but Dortmund handled it.

'When the gaffer was linked with us so heavily, I thought about the experience of that game and how positive everything around him and Dortmund felt. I was all in, and to be honest, a lot of the lads were desperate for it to happen. We knew his success with Dortmund was no accident and you could tell he was a special manager that could make a big difference.'

Carlo Ancelotti was the other candidate under consideration by FSG. While there was no questioning the Italian's pedigree as a three-time Champions League winner, he did not generate enthusiasm around the club. The owners were put off by his focus on rebuilding through transfers and he seemed to be more of an overseer of good teams rather than a constructor of one. The majority of players were of the belief that Ancelotti would want to secure success through immediate investment instead of attempting to bring the best out of them over time. The staff, meanwhile, had heard from colleagues within the game that the man who led Real Madrid to their 10th European Cup could be detached and didn't do much to uplift or inspire his squad or those behind the scenes.

'With Ancelotti, the general feeling was he wouldn't be the worst appointment because of his past accomplishments,' remembers one member of Liverpool's conditioning staff. 'But it was like you had to explain to yourself why he would be good for the job. It was the opposite with Klopp — everyone was bouncing around the place at the thought of him becoming the new manager, because it just made so much sense.'

The bulk of Liverpool's fanbase subscribed to the same thinking. They had been motioning on social media since 2014–15 for the German to take charge at Anfield under the 'Klopp for the Kop' tag and when it became clear he would succeed Rodgers, the boos and toxicity that marked the previous months were swept away by a groundswell of optimism.

There were three days between Rodgers' sacking and the confirmation of Klopp's appointment, which blitzed past in a blur. Klopp and Ulla had a flood of admin to take care of in a limited window, leaving little space to think about the job itself. 'We left a country and our lives there behind, if you want, so we had to organise a few things,' he explained. 'It was quite busy those few days, quite busy, and it was not a lot about football.'

Knowing the importance of supplying the right message from the off, Klopp downloaded a language app to ensure his communication in English was effective enough. If he was hoping for some quiet time to work on his opening gambits to the press, Liverpool's staff and his new players when he arrived on Merseyside, that plan was quickly stifled even before his departure from Germany.

A German television reporter buzzed Klopp's home hoping to snatch an exclusive interview via the intercom on 8 October and he wasn't disappointed. The broadcaster got one short sentence — 'from tomorrow, I will be a Liverpool man 24/7' — but that soundbite rippled across the world, with social media going into overdrive. Every bit of Klopp's journey from his home in Germany to Liverpool's John Lennon Airport was tracked, with the path of the private plane that was carrying him, his family and coaching assistants from Dortmund to Merseyside monitored in its entirety by over 35,000 people on Flightradar24.

As afternoon turned to evening, the roads leading to Liverpool's Hope Street Hotel were swarming with supporters waiting to welcome him. 'A party atmosphere' is how Klopp recalls it and while he was pleased with the reception, it was no fun having his privacy impeded by the paparazzi who also stationed themselves close to the boutique accommodation used by Liverpool ahead of home matches.

As he settled into the Rooftop Suite, Klopp could hear the sound of shutters and see the flashes of light but couldn't understand how it was possible for the photographers to get pictures into his room given it was so high up. Venturing out onto the private terrace, Klopp got his answer: they had made their way up adjacent buildings, hanging off the awnings to get their shot. He couldn't understand it: he was just a football manager about to take charge of a new club. Granted, it was one of the biggest and most historic football clubs in the game, but he couldn't fathom the fuss.

This was not just any managerial appointment though. It felt more symbolic. More than the start of a new tenure, the universal approval of Klopp offered a chance to unify the club, which would be imperative for success.

He was framed as a saviour, and in the hotel within walking distance of Liverpool's two cathedrals, he signed a three-year contract worth £7 million per season. The inking of the agreement took place in the hotel's Sixth Boardroom, with the steel outline of the new Main Stand at Anfield visible in the distance.

Klopp's task extended beyond an on-pitch regeneration; he would need to oversee advancement off it too. While FSG were in no doubt he was the perfect fit to achieve that, the length of the deal — eschewing the usual five-year term — was rooted in realism rather than romanticism. Klopp had never lived outside of Germany, let alone managed in a different country or at a club as demanding and unforgiving as Liverpool. He was conscious of Ulla needing to settle and her happiness on Merseyside. It was a big adjustment on an individual level for both of them but also for their marriage.

The official announcement of Klopp's signing was made by Liverpool at 9 pm, but by then the new manager was at an introductory dinner with Melwood staff. The expectation was that it was his chance to lay down the law and spell out his requirements for how things would work at the training ground going forward. Instead, it was the complete opposite.

'The gaffer asked us to explain how things are, what

we do, what he needed to learn,' goalkeeper coach John Achterberg, who has been at the club since 2009, remembers. 'He wanted to know more about us and how our departments worked and he listened to us. He asked us about the league, about rules, training schedules, how matchdays went. It was a good talk that showed us immediately that the gaffer was a team player. He didn't come in with the attitude that he knew everything. He told us the club could only achieve our ambitions if we did it all together and with the highest standards.'

Later that evening, Klopp toasted his new life with Ulla, their sons Marc and Dennis and his long-term assistant Peter Krawietz at The Old Blind School bar and restaurant. As the pints flowed, so too did the pictures and requests for autographs. His disguise of a cap and black hoodie was certainly not enough to mask the identity of the most popular man in Liverpool.

If the full scale of excitement around his appointment didn't dawn on Klopp yet, it would the next morning at his unveiling. Press from around the globe packed into the Reds Lounge at Anfield, with no place to stand let alone sit. A sea of cameras dominated the back section of the room, while photographers lay in the aisles and sprawled in front of the top table.

Considering the absence of preparation time as well

as the fact he had to deliver his messaging in a second language, it was staggering how surgically and effectively Klopp addressed all his key constituents. He told his new Liverpool 'family' there was no need to pull together big speeches — if he believed in what he was saying, so too would the people he needed to.

The first important group to address was the players and as the media attempted to extract negativity about the squad he inherited, he countered, 'I'm here because I believe in the potential of the team. I'm not a dream man, I don't want to have Cristiano Ronaldo or Lionel Messi and all these players in one team. I want this squad, it was a decision for these guys. Now we start working.'

The recruitment staff that struggled to share common ground with Brendan Rodgers were relieved to hear Klopp shut down talk of trouble with transfer decisions being made collaboratively. 'If two smart, intelligent, clever guys sit together on a table and you both want the same, where can be the problem? We all want to be successful,' he said. 'I'm not a genius, I don't know more than the rest of the world, I need other people to get me perfect information and when we get this we will sign a player or sell a player.'

Klopp took aim at the British press too, imploring them not to portray him as a messianic figure. 'Does anyone in this room think that I can do wonders?' he asked before answering, 'I'm a normal guy from the Black Forest. I'm the normal one. I hope to enjoy my work. Everyone has told me about the British press. It's up to you to show me they are all liars!'

The most significant point of his opening press conference was targeted at everyone associated with Liverpool including the supporters. 'History is only the base for us,' Klopp said. 'It is all the people are interested in, but you don't take history in your backpack and carry it with you for 25 years. We have to change from doubters to believers. We can write a new story if we want.'

Those final two lines were simplistic, but that was by design. It was vital that the message was clear, easy to digest and share. The club's silverware-lined history and the weight of expectation to deliver the league title had become a noose for previous managers. Klopp walked in and signalled his spell would not be dictated by it, which was different.

Adam Lallana remembers a few of the players watching the unveiling and being blown away by his courage to immediately tackle the 'weight of the badge, the weight of history, the weight of waiting so long for the title'. He labelled it a 'chest out' moment for the group.

'The gaffer could just see that pressure on everyone's shoulders and that's probably what shocked him the most when he first met everyone at the club, especially the players,' Lallana says. 'What was great and helped lift it is that he wasn't just talking to us about that. He spoke to the media about that from day one. There would be games that I'd see him turn around in the dugout, screaming at fans saying, "Why the hell are you having a go? What are you complaining for?" He'd be correcting the behaviour of fans to be more supportive while the game was going on and — just wow! As players, it was huge to see that and there was a collective feeling of, "Oh my god, he's got all our backs." We could tell from the beginning we got in just the kind of personality that was needed to make Liverpool successful.'

Long before Klopp's breakthrough in professional football with Mainz, he explored England via rail for a month. He swapped between sleeping in youth hostels, which offered free accommodation if he cleaned his room, and places that charged £5 as their bed-and-breakfast rate.

'The weather was not too good, but I love this country,' Klopp rewound. 'I loved the language, it didn't seem too difficult, and I was interested in meeting new people and learning their ways. I always knew I wanted to live here if it was possible. When I became a manager, it was clear that if there was a good opportunity in this country, to go for it.'

He did. And while Klopp's initial contract in England was for three years to assess his adjustment, just eight months into his tenure he remarked to Mike Gordon that he could imagine being at Liverpool for the rest of his managerial career.

That information was relayed to John Henry and Tom Werner, with FSG getting on the phone to Marc Kosicke and thrashing out terms of a new six-year deal. Klopp was on holiday in Ibiza before ferrying over to Formentera, the smallest of Spain's Balearic islands. On 16 June, as he celebrated his 49th birthday, he committed his future to the club until 2022. It was 'the best present' Klopp could have asked for as he was sure something special was brewing at Liverpool under his guidance. The team's identity was unmistakable and their ascent had begun. They had lost the League Cup and Europa League finals — but getting to them was the most important takeaway. Their trajectory was clear.

In December 2019, Klopp agreed another extension, this time until 2024. Liverpool were champions of Europe at that stage, but the manager predicted it was only the beginning. 'This is a statement of intent, one which is built on my knowledge of what we as a partnership have achieved so far and what is still there for us to achieve,' he said.

Liverpool would go on to become the first team in British history to hold the European Cup, domestic league title, Club World Cup and the Super Cup simultaneously.

Hitting for the cycle indeed.

3

A Change In Psychology

'When you agree on a common idea and work towards it together, you can create something very special. We are at a club that helps us now. That wasn't always the case. When I came here, the size of the club was a burden. Now it's our safety net, it's our trampoline, it's our home, it's our basis, it's everything to us. Now we are Liverpool, before the club was Liverpool and we were just the guys who were trying to be good enough.'

Jürgen Klopp

In the window behind Jürgen Klopp, spectacular greenery crawls up and coats the imposing, impressive Steinernes Meer mountain. There is a glimpse too of a glorious aquamarine lake, but it is not this unreal view that most pleases him. The Liverpool manager has delighted in seeing the self-belief and sense of belonging imbued in his players, which is in contrast to the broken bunch he found when he arrived at the club.

As he undertakes his fifth pre-season in charge — held in idyllic Austria — Klopp circles back to his first week on Merseyside when it was obvious that not many people thought much about the squad, including the team themselves.

'I came in and all the questions were straightaway, "Who will you sign?" And "Who will you sign?" is only because people think with these players you can't achieve anything,' he says. 'But I signed the contract because I thought, "Oh, that's a good team." Not a perfect one obviously, but it's a really good team with talent, with character, that needs direction. As soon as I came in, I realised nobody is happy with the team. And I realised the team is not happy with the team. That is a big, big problem and I thought, "Okay, this needs a proper restart." I needed the time to convince the boys about their own qualities and thankfully I was given the time and look at them now: champions of Europe, England and the world.'

Klopp is a process manager and that was exactly the tonic Liverpool needed in 2015: a figure with a clear plan of how to remedy the problems that haunted the club, especially the psychology of the place.

The Reds had not won the league for 25 years when

he joined, and it had been a decade since the Miracle of Istanbul, when the club won a fifth European Cup under Rafael Benitez's guidance. In 2006, an FA Cup was secured and in 2001 that trophy was also in the cabinet along with the UEFA Cup, League Cup and Super Cup under Gerard Houllier's charge. The Frenchman delivered another League Cup in 2003, with Kenny Dalglish adding that piece of silverware again in 2012.

The 1990s were bleaker, with a return of just one FA Cup (1992) and one League Cup (1995). In the 25 years without the holy grail prior to Klopp's appointment, there had been four second-placed finishes for Liverpool, each followed by a seismic crash. The weight of not winning the league always hit hardest when the team were so close, and as the years passed, the enormity of the wait clouded the club. Liverpool's golden history had become a gigantic noose stifling the present and it seemed inescapable.

Klopp had identified this as the greatest issue to solve before he had even arrived in the city. He could see it in the body language of the players during the stack of games he analysed and through the neurosis of the crowd. Heads dropped too quickly and there was a constant sense of inadequacy from those on the pitch and frustration from those in the stands. It is why it was the first subject he addressed during his interview with LFCTV after being announced as the club's new manager. 'We need to feel the confidence and the trust of the people,' Klopp said. 'It is important that the players feel the difference from now on, that they can reach the expectations.'

When he walked into Melwood, he realised the psychological state of the players was even worse than he had feared. 'The players were obviously listening to all the voices saying they are not good enough for the club or that I can't wait to get rid of them,' Klopp says. 'There were a lot of insecure players. I think, especially in England, everybody is used to the first thing a manager does to save his own life is to sack whoever he can. And by the way, I learned that not only the players think like this, it was in all departments. When I walked through the offices, I thought, "Okay, they don't believe that I'm actually here to work together with them and not try to find out who I was going to sack so that we can become be successful." I didn't think for a second about who I can get rid of. I needed a while so we could create this kind of really trustful relationship. And I think most departments still have the same people that were at the club before I came in.

'That's what I really like because it was not about the quality of the people, it was about other things. Finding a way, believing in the way, working for it and doing it all together. So we needed to create a bond at Melwood, but also especially with our supporters. Anfield is absolutely powerful. It's very, very influential. The atmosphere was not good before I arrived and it became a little bit better when I came in because of the excitement of someone new. But then with the first wrong pass it was again, "Oh my God, what's going on here?" So we had to change that.'

Klopp had to focus on fixing the confidence internally before he could properly influence external change. If the players and staff operated with conviction, it would automatically coax more out of supporters. He set about ensuring that his enthusiasm for Liverpool filtered through at his unveiling. Klopp underlined that he would never have accepted the job if 'I see the team and think, "Oh my God . . . no, no, no." In this moment, we are not the best team in the world — who cares?

'Who wants to be the best team in the world today? We want to be the best team tomorrow or another day. That's all. What I saw from outside is absolutely okay. I saw some good matches and some not so good, but it's normal in football you have some problems. You have to solve them.

'The important thing is we have speed, we have technical skills, we have tactical skills, we have good defenders, good midfielders, good strikers, wingers. I'm here because I believe in the potential of the team.'

The players, the majority of whom had been away on international duty when Klopp's appointment was made official, were digesting every word. 'There was a huge lift watching his first interview, then his press conference and reading everything he had said,' Jordan Henderson recalls. 'His presence, what he was saying and how he was saying it made me feel like he was excited to work with us, which gives you a boost as player.'

When the entire squad were back at Melwood, Klopp called his first major meeting. After inviting each member of staff at the training facility to introduce themselves and describe their roles to the players, it was time to spell out what he expected from the team. Conscious of bombarding them with too much information 'because it's like you're filling a glass with a bucket and that doesn't work very well', he went for a simple, yet impactful approach.

On a flipchart, he wrote out the word TEAM in capital letters and affixed a description to each initial on what he expected Liverpool to be.

T – TERRIBLE
E – ENTHUSIASTIC
A – AMBITIOUS
M – MENTALLY-STRONG MACHINES

A CHANGE IN PSYCHOLOGY

'I remember I wrote in big letters on a paper the word "TEAM" and I said that is what I want us to be,' Klopp explained on his third anniversary at the club.

'I said "T" is for terrible to play against — I had not a better word unfortunately . . . I don't know if I have a better one now. "E" for enthusiastic. "A" for ambitious. "M" for mentally-strong machines.

'Sometimes, we are exactly that! We can be terrible opponents to face, we have this kind of excited — a bit crazy if you want — style with organisation. We are for sure very enthusiastic and very ambitious and we have become stronger and stronger mentality-wise. Pretty much all of my players work like machines too, so I have actually what I wanted.'

One of Klopp's opening instructions to the team was to only pay attention to criticism from him and the coaches because 'it makes no sense to trust what people who are not involved in the process think', but it took a while for that message and for his conviction in the players to resonate. During the pre-season tour of Hong Kong in 2017, the Reds boss was still bemoaning the fragile psychology of the squad.

On the final day of 2016, Liverpool had beaten Manchester City and were second in the league, six points behind Antonio Conte's Chelsea. Transformed by the speed, directness and excellent decision-making of Sadio Mane, with Gini Wijnaldum providing extra tactical nous and Philippe Coutinho developing into a world-class footballer, the team made a blinding start to Klopp's first full campaign in charge. Arsenal were edged 4–3 on an opening day epic at the Emirates, Leicester were rinsed 4–1 in the first Anfield game featuring the new Main Stand, Chelsea were overcome at Stamford Bridge, Tottenham were bettered on Merseyside and Mane crushed Everton hearts on 94 minutes at Goodison Park ahead of the festive fixtures.

Liverpool were shaping up to be Chelsea's biggest title threat, but they shed that status in the new year.

Klopp broke down that period at the OZONE sky bar on the 118th floor of Hong Kong's grandiose Ritz-Carlton hotel. 'I would say we were completely confident until 31 December when we played Manchester City,' he told *Goal*. 'It was an outstanding battle for both sides with the 1–0 deserved, but anything could have happened in that match.

'Two days later, we played against Sunderland, a completely different game, but that was a draw. They are a deep-defending side, but twice we got past them and they needed two penalties to get a point, but immediately afterwards there was the feeling from the players of, "Oh, maybe we're not good enough. We've wasted our chance. We had the situation and we didn't use it."

'It was only one game! Everybody gave points away, even Chelsea — okay, not too often because they were champions at the end, but it happened. It's all about how you handle these situations and it's something we are really working on to be stronger in.

'We had two major issues in January [2017] obviously: not enough confidence as we should have had in ourselves, and too many injuries plus Sadio being away at the Africa Cup of Nations while the games didn't seem to stop.

'Then in February, we suffered from the intensity of the month before, and we were back in March. We won games again, but then people were saying, "It's not the same football, they are struggling", and this again gave the players doubt.

'They listen to these voices, the whole club listens to these voices that go, "Oh, it's again like this, they don't have Plan B for deep-defending sides, they can only play one way."

'We smashed teams at the start of last season by altering our style in different ways to play to our strengths and minimise the opposition's like against West Brom at Anfield. We limited their set-piece situations, which we know they are really dangerous from.

'The talk of Plan B shows a lack of understanding. In the moment when you are not feeling confident, you cannot change too many things — that's insecurity.

'It's not about showing what you can do – like "Hey, here is Plan D, F, Q!" My job is not to prove that I can do a thousand different techniques or no-looking coaching or whatever, it is to do what is best for the players I have, with our skills, in the situation we are in.

'When I hear or read these things about us, I know that 100 per cent I do not listen. But, oh my god, everybody else listens, so we have to block that out and focus on us and our way.

'Players make the right decisions when they have confidence, when they don't have it, then they feel "the next pass needs to be the goal" or "now we are under pressure and need to force it". No! You stick to what you're doing, try, try and try again. Each missed chance is not a failure, it is information — use it and go again.'

Liverpool's faith in themselves was a step-by-step process aided by superb performances and results, evolving together and adding greater quality to the squad — especially through the spine of the team with Mane, Mo Salah, Virgil van Dijk, Fabinho and Alisson. But Henderson stresses that Klopp is owed the biggest chunk of credit.

'He came in and changed the mood, the feeling around the place and the feeling we had about ourselves,' the captain says. 'He was conditioning us physically with really demanding, intense training sessions like we'd never known before, but he was also conditioning us mentally. A big thing of his was our mental state within games. The West Brom one at Anfield always sticks out because it just shows how he had the full picture in his head and works with that even if its questioned. A lot of people looked at us walking towards the Kop saluting the fans after a draw and went, "Well, what the hell is going on here?" Even as players you might be thinking, "This is odd." But he's always thinking differently. He's always looking at the bigger picture and in that game, he could start to see the change of mentality from us and the fans.

'It was really important because he would drill into us that a football game is 90 minutes, so if you're losing and they still have 20 minutes left, it's all about body language for him. If you lose momentum within a game, people's body language may change. Or even if you take the lead, your body language can change and you might drop deeper. He always pushed us to be on the front foot and keep going, no matter what the score is and no matter what stage of the game is. He'd say, "That's who we are, we'll keep going and going and going right until the referee blows his whistle." It wasn't, "Go and be all-out attack", he wanted us to control a game our way and not let the game happen to us. I can remember him being really assertive and repetitive with that kind of message.

'And in the West Brom game, because we went behind but kept searching for the equaliser and made it 2–2 so late, he liked the reaction. He could see a shift in the mentality and with the body language of the players. It's what he wanted to see and we worked on getting better with our reactions and that kind of resilience has just carried on. It became natural within the team. We were among the best teams in the Premier League this season for scoring in the last 10 minutes of games. And you can see whether we're scoring a goal or conceding, he wants us to react in a positive way. He has really drove that into the team over the past few years and it's been a key reason we've been successful.'

Klopp's first full campaign in charge ended with Liverpool having a crack at Champions League football again. Henderson reveals that before the manager had reached his first anniversary at the helm, players were discussing how they were destined to win trophies under him.

'The League Cup and Europa League finals came in his first few months and already it was obvious that our process was much better, our way was working and we were getting where we wanted to be and just had to build towards that final step,' he says. 'I just had this feeling that we were closing in on success and a lot of lads felt the same. We'd talk about it and we knew with this manager, with the staff at Melwood, with the character and quality of the players we have in the squad as well as how much work we were all willing to put in, that we created something special. It was a matter of time until we'd be winners. I felt that deep, deep down. Even after big defeats like Kiev, I knew we were on track to lift trophies.

'Did I think we're going win the Champions League, Super Cup, Club World Cup and Premier League in a year? No. Or that we'd get 97 points last season and then 99? Probably not either. But I always felt something was coming. I remember having conversations with people in 2017 about this, about how he completely changed the mentality around everything — and that's not just with the players, you could see the fanbase really responding to him and to us. It felt like we were building into one strong unit without a ceiling.'

While Liverpool's stellar recruitment during the Klopp era has indisputably elevated the team's self-belief with Van Dijk and Alisson offering greater surety, and as such, confidence in defence, the manager has been at pains to stress the club's advancement is down to the collective.

'We have brought in new players, but they alone cannot change everything,' he said in October 2018. 'We all need to remember this. I know what people think about Virgil van Dijk — he is a fantastic boy and a world-class player, but he did not sort our defensive problems on his own. Football does not work like that. Just like how Alisson cannot keep 500 clean sheets in a row by himself. The game does not make that possible.

'We have developed, kept the majority of the team together and made a few, strong adjustments. Our process has been step-by-step. You cannot give everyone a book, where you write all your requirements down and players read it and immediately understand it. You have to feel it, you have to do it plenty of times over and over on the training ground and you have to get used to it.'

Pep Lijnders picks out Klopp's ability to find the right words at the worst times as one of the core reasons for Liverpool's remarkable mental development. 'One thing is the ability to speak when you win,' the assistant manager says. 'What is much harder is the ability to touch on exactly the right things when you've just lost. He goes straight to the heart of the players. He can change perspectives. For me, that's what a true leader is: someone who shapes a team, but especially the psychology and character of the players. He has made them so much better prepared for ups and downs in football, but also in life.'

That sentiment is echoed by John Achterberg. 'He builds a club,' the goalkeeper coach says. 'But the boss also builds people. He changed how everyone sees themselves, and how people see us.'

Another element flagged by the players is the confidence they've derived from Klopp having their backs. One such insistence was when he took a stand against an insane fixture schedule, declining to let any senior players feature in the FA Cup fourth-round replay against Shrewsbury in February 2020, which coincided with the mid-season break he had promised the squad for their relentless efforts. He was pilloried for the decision by pundits, the press and the opposition, but it was massively appreciated in Liverpool's dressing room.

The way Klopp had protected Coutinho after Liverpool refused to accede to his transfer request in the summer of 2017, only selling him to Barcelona for £142 million the following January, also drew great respect from the players. The aggrieved playmaker was unavailable for selection at the start of the season due to a 'back injury' that was heckled and met with inverted commas each time it was mentioned. Klopp never deviated from that line — even when the player turned out for Brazil and the national team doctor said the issue was 'only emotional'. Squad harmony was prioritised by Klopp, who did not mind being the subject of ridicule to preserve it.

Conversely, the team had also learned that there

would be no tolerance for a player who showed a lack of respect for the rules. That schooling was provided by Mamadou Sakho. The French centre-back was not involved in the 2016 Europa League final after copping a Uefa doping charge that was later dismissed after it was established that no rules had been broken. That summer, Liverpool travelled to the United States for their pre-season tour, but the French centre-back delayed the flight out, having arrived late to travel.

While in Palo Alto, he didn't show up to a recovery session, which impacted the schedule of physios and he also joined a team meal well after it had started. Klopp sent him home from the USA, not wanting that kind of attitude around the place. 'I have to build a group here and we've got to start new here,' the manager explained at the time. 'We have some rules and we have to respect them — if somebody gives me the feeling they are not respecting it I have to react.'

Sakho continued to be a problem that September, going on a 3 am Snapchat rant about being frozen out of the first-team and hurling accusations about lies. The defender was exiled from squad and trained with the Academy players before joining Crystal Palace on a loan deal which was then made permanent. That was the first and last repeated rule breach by a player under Klopp.

'When the boss came in, he made it clear we have to move in the same direction together,' Achterberg says. He told the boys, "I need you all and I want to be your friend, but I cannot be your best friend." Anyone who wanted to give their best was welcomed with open arms, but if you didn't want to, he would give you a kick up the arse. If you didn't want to train at the highest level and respect his way — goodbye. But if you want to be a part of this special story, everyone is treated the same whether you start every week or are one of the kids.'

This was evidenced by how incensed Klopp was when he was informed that a minimum of five top-flight appearances needed to be made in order for a player to qualify for a Premier League winners' medal. And not the first time he was riled by the complete misunderstanding of the importance of the entire squad in terms of creating a culture of excellence and maintaining the highest standards.

'I really hate it when people from outside don't understand this,' Klopp says. So we become English champions, and in the moment when you think you have no problems, that you've finally done it, someone comes and tells you, "Oh, he won't get a medal and he won't get a medal and he won't get one." That is a massive problem to me. I think how silly can you be that you now want to decide after having nothing to do with what we achieve here who can get a medal? I really hate that. We had that at the Club World Cup. People told me, "So you go there on the stage, but these ones won't get anything." So I said, "Okay. What I will do, I will go there and when the Sheikh or whoever wants to give me a medal, I won't take it. Tell them I will kill the whole ceremony. Make sure they are all going to get a medal, or we don't come for it and they can celebrate themselves." I just don't understand how these things can happen. It's really important and it's not that people want these medals, it's that they deserve it and should get it.'

Klopp has urged football's authorities to lift their limitations on rewarding full squads for their feats. With Liverpool geared to win more silverware under the German, it would him save a lot more exasperation should they listen.

At his unveiling, Klopp declared, 'I am not the guy who is going to shout, "We are going to conquer the world!"' and yet that is what Liverpool have done on his watch. 'Please give us time to work on it,' he requested. 'If you want, this could be a really special day.' The patience and the process — to which the change of psychology was central — has paid off in kind.

4

Method Over Money

'What you need and what they [Liverpool] have is
a team with a full understanding of the club,
working towards the same goal through use of a
variety of data and knowledge to make informed
decisions.'

David Sumpter, author of Soccermatics

Three years before Jürgen Klopp became manager of
Liverpool, two pivotal months would shape the platform he'd have to lead the team back to the promised
land. In March 2012, Fenway Sports Group president
Mike Gordon officially assumed control of the
day-to-day operations of the club, a vision principal
owner John W Henry had pitched the previous
summer.

His first day on the job was flooded with meetings

held in Florida and one in particular had a lasting impact. At Henry's lakefront estate in Boca Raton, the venue for the business talks, Gordon met Michael Edwards. They shared a love of data, a loathing of the limelight, a laidback approach and a devotion to finding the edges in a football market largely dominated by the wealth of oligarchs and sheikhs.

The following month, the pair combined for a masterstroke. Liverpool had been trying to lure the services of Decision Technology from Tottenham (a company that curated customised data analysis for European clubs, which provided a framework for player recruitment and squad optimisation selections, since 2010; they also developed the Castrol Index, a novel player-rating system used at both Euro 2008 and the World Cup in South Africa). That was legally tricky to pull off so Gordon and Edwards changed tack, directly hiring the stats company's greatest mind, Dr Ian Graham, to become director of research.

To understand the success of the Klopp era is to understand these key figures, who all shun the public eye but have been absolutely pivotal to Liverpool's restoration. 'From an operations point of view, this is exactly how I think it should work, that different brains throw their knowledge together, and in the end, reach the right decision for the club,' Klopp says.

The relationship between Klopp, Gordon and

Edwards, which the German tags 'absolutely incredible on a professional and personal level' is described as the 'holy trinity' at Liverpool. They discuss and decide on every major football decision, supported largely by industry-leading insights from Graham's research team, in the most casual way possible.

All three men can't be bothered with suits or stuffy meetings or overcomplicating matters. The trio often talk through the biggest issues — whether it be blockbuster transfers or a development with the new training ground — over breakfast or lunch. Gordon stays over at Klopp's house in Formby when he visits from Boston, as was the case after Liverpool's Champions League victory parade in 2019 and that December to seal the manager's new five-year contract.

FSG's president and the second-largest stakeholder in a multi-billion dollar conglomerate that owns two of sport's great brands in Liverpool FC and the Boston Red Sox, may be based in the capital of Massachusetts but he keeps in daily contact with Klopp, Edwards, CEO Billy Hogan and all other key stakeholders at the club.

Gordon, who grew up in Milwaukee, Wisconsin, lost his father to lung cancer when he was just 17 and in the process of selecting his higher education institution. As an avid baseball lover, Tufts University was just the ticket given its 15-minute drive away from the storied

Fenway Park, home of the Red Sox. He graduated with high honours, earning a joint degree in classical studies and economics. An interest in analytics saw him apply to an entry-level programme for college undergrads at Fidelity Investments and broke into their equity research department.

Through a nine-year spell, Gordon thrived as he managed Fidelity's large-scale mutual funds, including its Blue Chip Growth Fund. Despite his ascent, he made friends and — remarkably — didn't alienate people in a ruthless industry. He was calm, calculated and comfortable with risk, which saw him garner considerable success and respect.

Gordon left Fidelity in 1996 to link up with his colleague Jeff Vinik, owner of the Tampa Bay Lightning ice hockey team. His work with the hedge fund Vinik Asset Management — at one stage managing more than $9 billion in assets — gave him an entry into sport and Gordon's influence in that sphere would soon balloon.

Not long after Henry and Tom Werner took over the Red Sox in 2002, they recruited him and Vinik as limited partners. The former made a lasting impression, increased his stake in FSG and when the company, then known as New England Sports Ventures, rid Liverpool of the ownership of Tom Hicks and George Gillett with a £300 million purchase on

15 October 2010, he would become fundamental to shaping the club.

The testimonies of Gordon's expertise and personality are illuminating. 'One of the best humans you could ever meet,' is how Vinik described him, pointing out that he is 'very smart, very thoughtful and really outstanding at solving problems and finding solutions to difficult issues'.

It is easy to see why Henry entrusted him with running Liverpool and why Klopp adores Gordon. 'With Mike, the relationship always was from the first day, outstanding,' he says. 'He has such a supportive nature and he works incredibly hard. It's impressive how he learnt everything about football, about getting the advantages, building a really strong club and how good he is with planning. On a personal level, the relationship is excellent.'

Like Gordon, Klopp also lost his dad, Norbert, to cancer with both men not getting a chance to share their career successes with their fathers. The duo have been the biggest donators to Edwards' fundraising for Prostate Cancer UK over the past five years. One of Gordon's major decisions at Liverpool was his backing of the sporting director and a collaborative, analytics-informed decision-making process. During Brendan Rodgers' time, the division that existed between him and the transfer committee was not only causing immediate, expensive mistakes, it was hampering FSG's long-term strategy for the club. The external noise was calling for Liverpool to dismantle the structure, but Gordon knew there was nothing wrong with the methodology — only the openness to the collegiate approach of the man leading it.

Edwards and the committee would stay, Rodgers would be sacked and Klopp — well versed in the continental model at both Mainz and Borussia Dortmund — was roped in to make it all tick. 'I remember in my first press conference, I was asked about the transfer committee,' Klopp says, still puzzled by why so many thought the construct was a problem. 'It makes absolute sense. I don't want to waste time with talking to different agents or going through all the numbers, I'm busy enough dealing with the players we have. So I'm really happy that this part of the job is not mine. I can't have and I don't want to have the responsibility of deciding how much we have to spend because I am not a finance guy. Somebody has to tell me how much money we have, that's good, that's how I like it. We throw in all the information and then we go and make what we think is the best decision.

'Michael [Edwards] is a brilliant sporting director and was pretty much doing the job already without that title — I hope he got more money! He is a really intelligent guy, just like Mike [Gordon], and we have open discussions about everything, which is how it should be.'

Edwards, or 'Eddie' as he is referred to at Melwood, has been crucial in helping recruit the squad of mentality monsters. Roberto Firmino, Mohamed Salah, Sadio Mane and Andy Robertson are some of the players he pushed particularly hard for, with the wisdom of Graham's research. Edwards' negotiation skills saw Liverpool sign Alisson Becker from Roma for £65 million, despite the Serie A side insisting his cost was £90 million at one point.

Edwards' office is across from Klopp's and both men employ an open-door policy, encouraging staff to walk in and fire away. Transfer discussions are always fluid, with the bulk of the homework on players carried out by Dave Fallows, the head of recruitment, chief scout Barry Hunter, head of football projects David Woodfine, as well as Graham's team.

A shortlist of targets, ordered by priority, is talked through with Gordon, who approves finances for the deals but also provides whatever support may be necessary. An example of that was how he smoothed relations with Southampton's hierarchy, who had accused Liverpool of tapping up Virgil van Dijk in June 2017, allowing the club to complete a world-record deal for the defender at the end of that year.

There is respect and appreciation among the trio for their roles in the recruitment process: stylistic fits are provided by Edwards, Klopp is the magnet that attracts the players and the man who improves them, while Gordon gets all the deals over the line.

Liverpool's net transfer spend for the last five years reads £89.79 million as of 31 August 2020, in contrast to £505.6 million for new rivals Manchester City and £378.9 million for their traditional foes Manchester United. While the club have bought well, they have also sold excellently, fetching over £367 million under Klopp's watch.

Kevin Stewart, a fringe player, practically funded the deal for Robertson, who has grown into one of the game's foremost left-backs. A trade with Hull City saw the midfielder move there for £8 million, with Liverpool paying a measly £2 million more for the Scotland captain.

The exit of Phil Coutinho was the most profitable at £142 million, but also the most taxing transfer to handle of the Klopp era. In July 2017, Liverpool's pre-season tour of Hong Kong was wrecked by monsoon conditions that lead to a series of cancelled training sessions. But the weather and missed workouts would quickly become the least of their worries. On 21 July, Klopp woke up in West Kowloon — seven hours behind the

UK — to messages from Gordon and Edwards relaying that the club had instantly rejected a £72 million bid from Barcelona for Coutinho, underlining that he was not for sale at any price.

The playmaker had signed a new five-year deal without a release clause that January, but it was Barça who had come calling and his head was turned. At breakfast at the Ritz-Carlton that morning, Klopp scheduled a chat with Coutinho for the evening to hear his thoughts. It was an honest and respectful dialogue: Liverpool could not lose a key component of the squad so close to the new season just because the Catalans were not prepared for Paris Saint-Germain coming in for Neymar, but the player countered by saying he'd have to put his family's wishes first.

Klopp understood the Brazilian's dilemma, but repeated that he'd have to prioritise the club's ambitions. On 11 August 2017, Liverpool officially put that position out to the world. 'We wish to offer clarity as regards our position on a possible transfer of Philippe Coutinho,' read a statement on the club's official website, emphasising their 'definitive stance is that no offers for Philippe will be considered and he will remain a member of Liverpool FC when the summer window closes'.

Liverpool stuck to that despite the player's transfer request and the usual tactics when trying to force a move. If it was solely Klopp's choice, he'd have sanctioned Coutinho's sale before the start of the 2017–18 season, having seen how pained the player was. The manager ultimately supported the reasoning of Edwards, Gordon and the ownership group in general, and it was he who was targeted in the press offensive by the No 10's camp. Comments about the player's relationship with Klopp were unwelcome, especially as the Reds boss still publicly fought his corner and protected him.

The window closed and Coutinho's advisors still threatened his non-availability for Champions League games. Gordon and Edwards were tireless in working to remove that as an option and Klopp began re-integrating the star back into the squad.

His performances were stellar, but as the end of the year approached, it was clear Barça would return and the player was still set on a switch to Camp Nou. Klopp did not want to live through the upheaval of the summer again, but Liverpool were on the ascendancy and were concerned about risking their advancement by letting him go.

A very lucrative offer was made in an attempt to convince Coutinho to stay until the end of the season, even allowing him to strike a deal with Barça and join them ahead of the new campaign, but he would not budge. The orchestrator of Liverpool's play had given five years of service to the club and he felt it was time to say goodbye.

Gordon was concerned that selling Coutinho would cause unrest among the supporters at such a positive juncture. He wanted any bullets to be directed at the ownership rather than Klopp and advocated putting out an open letter explaining the reasons behind the sale. The manager, the calmest man at Melwood, dismissed that idea emphatically. He urged Gordon, Edwards and everyone else to relax; this was just another football transfer. If Liverpool did not want to invite drama around the decision, they should absolutely not create it themselves.

On 6 January 2018, a New Year's celebration that had long been pencilled in for Liverpool's staff at the Klopp residence in the Freshfield area of Formby coincided with Coutinho's £142 million exit to Barça. 'Players will come and players will go, that is football, but as a club we are big enough and strong enough to continue with our aggressive progression on the pitch, even when we lose an important player,' read the message on the club website completely scripted by the manager. 'We have never been in a better position in recent times, as a club, to react in the right way. We will use our size and strength to absorb moments like this and still move forward.'

At the party, there was a toast to Coutinho but also

defiance: better things were certain to come with or without him. The handling of the situation in its entirety showed Liverpool's new face: they would not be bullied by football's apex predators as was the case in the past, they would operate on their own terms and extract maximum buck — and importantly — they backed themselves to upgrade the squad. There would be no debilitation, no change to the upward direction. Klopp was sure of it and so everyone else was too — and he would be proved correct.

How Liverpool have mastered the market owes a lot to being industry pioneers in analytics. David Sumpter, a Professor of Applied Maths and author of *Soccermatics*, says they are 'some distance ahead of their competitors'.

Having studied the operating habits of clubs across the continent, he provided a succinct analysis of what marks Liverpool out from the competitors. 'What you need and what they have is a team with a full under-standing of the club, working towards the same goal through use of a variety of data and knowledge to make informed decisions,' he told the *Independent*.

'Liverpool are well run, properly structured and have a clear identity. Without this, it wouldn't matter how brilliant Ian Graham's work is.

'Not only do they have the right platform for their

data scientists to work, but they've empowered them and have great synergy in decision-making.

'There is no sole genius at Liverpool. It is not Graham or Klopp or Edwards — it is collection of all these superb minds coming together to meet objectives and generate success.'

Ignacio Palacios-Huerta, a Professor at the London School of Economics, who doubles up as a director of the football club Athletic Bilbao, has labelled Liverpool 'clear leaders' in using analytics to take crucial decisions, especially in the transfer market.

When FSG bought the club, it was expected that they would implant a similar data-driven approach at Anfield that restored the Red Sox to glory. Football analytics, however, were not as expansive, trusted in the sport or easy to find experts in. The owners plumped for Damien Comolli to become the club's director of football in November 2010 and while he didn't last at the club, he made one of its most important hires.

A year after joining Liverpool, he recruited Michael Edwards from Tottenham to do the football interpretation and video analysis. He was also brought in on account of having a sharp understanding of data and could judge whether methodology was solid or not. Comolli had gone to Ian Graham for recommendations and he circled Edwards, who was intelligent, open to new methods, but also critical of them — always posing questions of a model to ensure it could be properly applied to football.

His route into the industry was unique. Edwards grew up in Southampton and signed for Peterborough United in 1995 as a right-back who could also feature in the heart of defence or holding midfield. He was, as one source puts it, 'James Milner-esque in his professionalism', but 'was probably a better thinker of the game than player'. He was released two years later without having made a first-team appearance and enrolled at Peterborough Regional College before earning a degree in business management and informatics from the University of Sheffield. Edwards taught IT at a local high school in Peterborough but did not enjoy it and wanted to return to football. In 2003, Portsmouth signed a contract with Prozone and were after an analyst. Simon Wilson, a former teammate of Edwards, was in analytics at Southampton and pushed him for the role.

A meeting at a service station with Barry McNeill, who was Prozone's business development manager, led to Edwards joining Portsmouth under Harry Redknapp within a month in a first-floor office at Wellington Sports Ground. He was their opposition analyst, post-match analyst, scout and someone the players would go to for tips on how to improve their game.

Redknapp swapped Portsmouth for Tottenham in October 2008 and took Edwards with him a year later to become head of performance analysis and it wasn't long before Liverpool would come knocking.

Eddie is popular with staff and players at Melwood. Even though he is shrewd in the market, agents and managers around Europe hold him in high esteem. A scan of the supporters for his Prostate Cancer UK fundraising tells a story: beyond Klopp and Gordon, you'll find former Liverpool striker Daniel Sturridge, super agent Jorge Mendes, Raheem Sterling's representative Aidy Ward and a whole host of some of the most influential figures in the game.

Edwards made it his duty to ensure the club were at the forefront of analytics. The coup of pinching Graham's services in 2012 was instructive to the process. A doctor in the field of theoretical physics — he completed a PhD at the University of Cambridge in early 2005 — he was brought in to collect, organise and analyse bespoke data for the football side of the business, which Liverpool didn't have. Graham was starting from scratch, with recruitment the key area of his focus but he had the backing of the ownership group and Edwards.

Gordon was always proactively asking questions of Graham's research and the club believed if they were making one fewer mistake in the market — not spending £20 million on a player who didn't make an impact, for example — then the department was paying for itself. Building the tools for surgical recruitment was his first major task. Working initially under the supervision of Edwards but then on his own, Graham now runs a team of six. Will Spearman, who has a doctorate in particle physics from Harvard and worked for the European Organisation for Nuclear Research, is in charge of long-term, on-pitch research. His expertise is in pioneering new ways to analyse spatial models and developing pitch control. Spearman sparked Graham's interest through an Opta Pro analytics forum while employed by Hudl, who offer fully customisable performance data, where he studied player tracking. The Lead Data Scientist grew up in Texas, but says he's been made to feel at home at Liverpool.

Tim Waskett, who holds a first-class honours degree in astrophysics, was Graham's first hire. Former junior chess champion and energy industry professional Dafydd Steele completes the data science side of the team.

Mark Howlett and Mark Stevenson are responsible for the technology, maintaining the databases and building the research website. Their research now covers the academy, sharing insights with the sports science, medical and finance departments. The question is always, what data can Liverpool collect in every area and how can it help improve decision-making.

Spearman's work also informs the analysts and the coaching staff. Pre-match analysts James French and Greg Mathieson and their post-match counterparts

Harrison Kingston and Mark Leyland have access to a platform that allows them to view the research team's data on things like expected possession value models that are linked to video to guide their reports.

Many football clubs have an analytics department, but not all of them are empowered. There is still a high level of distrust in stats or a dismissive take on 'laptop nerds'. At Liverpool, traditional methods and a cutting edge have combined to powerful effect because as one source states 'there's a clear, strong decision-making process where the club wants to get as much information as possible from all the experts, rather than just wanting to check a box and say, "Oh, we have that." There hasn't been any turf guarding or fear of new approaches or new ways to look at things.'

Video alone and data on its own can be misleading, which is why Liverpool subscribe to a total, critical process. One of the club's standout players from 2019–20 had looked clumsy in many of the clips analysed before signing him. He would lose his balance often, or sky shots. The data, though, showed him to have all the qualities Liverpool were seeking for the position and the footage didn't really paint a full picture of the match situations.

One recruit that stood out in both the video and data breakdowns was Naby Keita, a midfield hybrid who is both a destroyer and a creator. A slow settling-in period and injuries have prevented the Guinea international from showcasing the extent of his brilliance, but his progressive numbers — how many of his actions led to positive events — already indicate how much of a difference he makes to Liverpool's front-foot play.

Amongst others, the research team's rigorous homework also informed the decision to hire Klopp, to discount Mohamed Salah's spell at Chelsea and sign him from Roma, and to wait on Van Dijk because no other centre-back was close to comparable. There are no pats on backs and feet up on desks. Models are continuously being built and improved for all sections of the club, from the fitness coaches to the commercial team, to assess whether they are making the most effective choices possible.

And the clarity of vision from Klopp, Gordon and Edwards makes it easy to design any kind of tool: transfer-wise for example, there is no confusion as to the profile of a Liverpool player. In this regard, one of Liverpool's fundamental improvements has been to drown out the noise.

Modern football has devolved into 'winning the transfer market', with winning matches no longer cutting it. Fans and pundits alike have become intoxicated by who can spend the most money and lure the most eye-catching names. The obsession with signings has led to fatalism — how could Liverpool possibly compete with United when they were signing the likes of Memphis Depay and Alexis Sanchez? How could they possibly win anything without Nabil Fekir?

The France international was pursued to fill the void left by Coutinho's departure and to inject some dynamism in the absence of the injured Alex Oxlade-Chamberlain. All the terms for a £53 million transfer were agreed with Lyon pending a medical, and given the short turnaround time, the attacker also did his introductory interview with LFCTV. However, the physical examination in Paris flagged an underlying knee issue — which made it irresponsible for Liverpool to continue with the deal. Fekir had suffered a cruciate ligament rupture in his right knee while on international duty in September 2015, requiring arthroscopic surgery to clean a joint in August 2016. He then suffered a contusion in the area in February 2018 and there was significant damage which left question marks over his durability over time.

Liverpool had spent years correcting poor market decisions of the past and making the right call was more important than appeasing fans.

Klopp, Edwards and Gordon have shunned football's buy or bust culture. Transfers centre around what the team requires rather than public opinion. After winning the title, the manager was asked about strengthening his team — a matter complicated by the ruinous financial effects of coronavirus.

Liverpool declined to follow through with a move for Timo Werner, who ended up at Chelsea, due to the uncertainty surrounding future income as well as the millions already lost. 'I am happy with my squad 100 per cent,' Klopp said. 'I was last year when people wanted us to sign him and him, but because of our reasons we did not do it. It's not that we don't want to, we try to make the right decisions constantly and then Covid-19 came. The situation changed and not for the better. It's not that we think we cannot improve with transfers, we do what is right for us and what we are able to do, that's all.

'If other teams invest I have no idea, they may know more about the future, I don't know. But the main difference between us and other teams this year was consistency. My boys are resilient like mad. We put absolutely everything into the games and that's what the difference was. I don't know if you can get that sort of thing on the transfer market. We had to build this and it's not about spending. It is about having the right team for the next season, based on your own situation.

'The club cannot buy just because other teams buy and everyone wants us to. We buy if we have the money for it and the need for it. If one of these things is not there we will not buy and we will go again. Imagine last year, 97 points and what would your recommendation have been to me transfer wise? Who should we have brought in to close the one-point gap to Manchester City? I don't even know who was available.

'There were a lot of recommendations out there I'm sure, but we didn't and you saw what happened. We will have a lot of tests next year, like we did this year and last year, we have to make sure we are ready. Some of them can be solved in the transfer market, but not all of them.'

Liverpool have been wise not to betray the principles that have seen them restored as a domestic and continental powerhouse. While there is an appreciation that there is a massive difference in being at the top versus playing catch-up trying to get there, there will be no wild shift of approach.

An unwavering dedication to their way has got the club this far and abandoning that would be counterproductive. Liverpool have proven that you do not always have to do the headline deal — Van Dijk and Alisson were exceptions given their status as certified gamechangers. Many of Liverpool's transfers have not been obvious. They were pilloried for advocating a £29 million deal for Firmino, buying 'Chelsea flop' Salah, overspending on Sadio Mane and settling for mediocrity by bringing in Robertson, Oxlade-Chamberlain and Gini Wijnaldum.

Liverpool find the edges, like activating Takumi Minamino's £7.5 million release clause before it was widely known and taking advantage of Xherdan Shaqiri's relegation exit clause of £13 million.

'The club have invested in the right people to make the right decisions,' captain Jordan Henderson says. It's hard to argue with that. It is the method rather than money that has put Liverpool back on its perch.

It is a seriously well-run club in all regards, with a hive of great minds coming together under a united purpose. There have, of course, still been own goals. The call to furlough around 200 staff as the world's seventh-richest football club in April 2020 may have had economic grounding, but it cut across Liverpool's 'This Means More' mantra and community responsibility. Klopp, Edwards and other high earners at Melwood along with the squad were willing to make wage sacrifices to ensure no one at the club lost their job. Fierce criticism of the club's decision from former players, supporters and the press forced a U-turn 48 hours later.

That had shades of the ticket price debacle in 2016, where £59 seats were increased to £77 in the redeveloped Main Stand. Supporters' groups organised a protest during the hosting of Sunderland on 6 February. Anfield witnessed its first walkout in history in the 77th minute, with 10,000 fans estimated to have filtered out of the stands.

FSG changed that decision within 24 hours, admitted their mistake and apologised. On the whole, the masterstrokes have greatly outweighed missteps and the club are healthier in every way, from their commercial expansion to their relationship with supporters as evidenced in events such as the BOSS Nights and the appointment of Liverpool's first fan liaison officer, the former *Times* writer and Scouser, Tony Barrett.

The progression on the pitch, meanwhile, has told in trophies.

In 2007, the Kraft Group, owners of the New England Patriots, had done due diligence on buying Liverpool. They were attracted by the history of the club, the scale of the global fanbase and the power of football. Those were good reasons to make the purchase, but there was a huge con: rivals were far better resourced, too much of a makeover was required across departments, supporters were too impatient and the expectation was not in keeping with reality.

Jonathan Kraft, the president of the group, admitted they did not have the confidence to rebuild Liverpool. Klopp, Gordon and Edwards, all ably supported by their staff, have succeeded where most others didn't even see the point in attempting it.

Even though Liverpool's owners are not as wealthy as their rivals — City's Sheikh Mansour is worth an estimated $20 billion, Chelsea's Roman Abramovich $11.3 billion, United's Glazer family $5 billion, while even the likes of Wolves (China's Fosun International, $5.6 billion), Villa (Egyptian Nassef Sawiris, $5.8 billion) and Crystal Palace (American Joshua Harris, $4.3 billion) dwarf FSG's net worth of $2.7 billion — they constructed a smart, sustainable and holistic way to achieve what seemed impossible.

'What we do here is we really believe in each other,' the manager says. 'People always thought that education only worked with warnings and shouting and being smacked. My education as a child was like that. No! Respect, faith, trust and creating a really good environment where everyone wants to contribute and play their part is what makes the difference. This is what works and this is what we have. We don't have random people at Liverpool, we have really smart ones and so you can put your belief fully into everyone. We work to make the right decision, and if we get it wrong, we talk and then we change it and try again to make the right one. There is no blame or whatever, we enjoy what we do and we enjoy doing it together. This is how you create a special atmosphere, where you are excited to come to work each day. I don't know if other clubs have this, but I hope they do. I have been lucky to have it at Mainz, Dortmund and now at Liverpool. I could not work any other way.'

5

Strengthening Off The Pitch

'The energy, the trust, it's like a small, close family even though it's such a big club.' *Pep Lijnders*

On an upper floor of Melwood, on the wall that links Jürgen Klopp's office to that of his coaches, there is a portrait of the manager made up entirely of the names of every single employee at the training base. The manager is particularly fond of the artwork, which is adjacent to framed photographs of the other men who have led the club throughout its history. Klopp is the face of Liverpool's revival, but the symbolism of being sketched using all the other individuals at the complex feeds into his constant reminder that 'I am not a one-man show. I have never been that in my life and I will never be that.'

Throughout his career in football, both as a player

and in the technical area, Klopp has stressed the importance of the collective. The concept of togetherness is why he opted for football over tennis and the other individual winter sports he also excelled at, explaining, 'I want to be a member of something bigger.'

Along with the training pitches that office wall, which also features large group pictures taken since 2018 of each person who reports to Liverpool's 'football HQ' — from Virgil van Dijk to the janitor, Mick Bibby — is Klopp's favourite part of the facility. It circles back to core messages he delivered during his first major meeting as the club's manager: 'you cannot be the best team on the pitch without having the best team off it' and 'everyone is responsible for everything'.

Assistant manager Pep Lijnders remembers the 'unbelievable energy' of that opening presentation, which made the staff at Melwood 'feel like giants'. Having joined during the international break, Klopp used his initial days in the job to learn about everyone that worked at the complex in West Derby and when the players returned from representing their countries, he gathered the squad in the press conference room for his introductory address.

Before he could spell out what he expected of the team, there was something more important to do. Klopp invited each member of staff at Melwood to walk in, describe a little bit about themselves and detail their roles to the group. He then told the players that every person that came into the room was dedicating their days to helping Liverpool perform to their maximum.

'It was a key reminder to them, to create responsibility, to show how many people are working in the background to make sure they only have to think about training,' Lijnders says. For goalkeeping coach, John Achterberg, it was also a sign to the training ground employees that they were crucial to the club attaining success.

'He wanted to make it clear the way he thinks and the way he wants to work, where everyone is involved and it is one big team,' the Dutchman explains. 'For Jürgen, there is no separation between the players and staff or between the groundsmen, cleaners or coaches – everyone is important. He always says improvement can't only come in one area, it has to happen across the club. If each person walks in with the idea of being the best they can be, that makes the club stronger. Everyone felt part of the process of making Liverpool the best team in the country again after that meeting, and look what has happened.'

The relationship between the players and staff at Melwood has always been one based on respect, but those who have experienced the setup for over two decades believe the mutual appreciation, buy-in and trust has been enormously strengthened under Klopp.

There is no longer a sense of separation under the 'we are one, we are Liverpool' policy. And there is no space for, as one of the backroom team put it, the 'blame culture' which used to be prevalent before.

Achterberg pinpoints the 'willingness to take owner-ship for errors and drops in standards' as one of the biggest differences in the building. 'The focus is now "what could have I done better?"' he says, 'instead of "well, why didn't X do that better?" The whole vibe around the place and the way of working has changed.'

That was deliberate from Klopp. Having a happy environment at the hub of Liverpool's football prepar-ation was ultimately paramount for success, but also for how well he settled into his first job and life-changing experience out of Germany. The training centre was where he would spend a minimum of 10 hours daily and Klopp wanted to look forward to going into the place every day — and he wanted all the other employees to feel the same.

To achieve that, he had to give them a sense of belonging to the process, which was sparked by his big address. Klopp was also forceful on pencilling-in regular socials and lengthy away trips together so bonds were established on a personal level rather than just profes-sionally.

Invitations to gatherings were previously restricted which led to conflict, division and feelings of not being worthy enough to get the nod. The kitchen team and receptionists, for example, were excluded and it was only ever the direct football staff that would consistently get the chance to attend. That culture was immediately eradicated under Klopp.

'When he came in, there was this immediate shift of positive energy and doing away with a lot of things that caused friction at Melwood,' says Danielle McNally. As the manager's personal assistant, she is central to planning these get-togethers along with Ray Haughan, the general manager of first-team operations. Trip arrangements, meanwhile, are expertly dealt with by travel department head, Phil Holliday, and his deputy Andy McDonald.

'Jürgen's big thing was we are one, we are Liverpool, we are together,' McNally adds. 'When he did the introduction of every single member of staff to the players during his first meeting, we knew it was going to be different. And then, he booked a meal for everyone in the building at Fazenda restaurant in the city centre. There wasn't anyone left out and that was really the start of the closeness because any of the divisions that used to exist were gone.

'We had another gathering at Hope Street not long after that where it was again open to all the staff and it was obvious that it would be how things worked going forward. It's amazing that he just walked through the door and instantly knew what to do to ensure things were better and people feel better. It's not just an invitation to events either; Jürgen has the ability to make everyone feel important. He lets you know when you're doing a good job, he loves to see you enjoying yourself, he takes a genuine interest in you and that has such a huge effect on the people and around the place.'

Regular gatherings became the norm and Liverpool's warm weather training camps in Tenerife from 2016 to 2018 also served as team-building exercises that extended to the staff and their families. Partners and kids were welcomed with Klopp's wife, Ulla, for example, really taking to canteen duo, Carol Farrell and Caroline Guest, who are motherly figures at Melwood.

With the complex reserved for employees only — a change the manager made when he arrived to keep it focused on football without guests always hanging around as a distraction, which was the case in the past — it was vital to enable a connection aside from work. 'The Christmas parties, which could be stuffy before, became one of the things we most looked forward to,' McNally says, remembering scenes of Klopp on the dancefloor, in the photo booth or simply sitting and soaking up the joy of others.

'The trips to Tenerife were massive in pulling everybody together. The families got to feel part of our work and see things from the inside, which was so helpful. It was also a "thank you" from the manager to the staff for their hard work and a nice way of giving back to our loved ones for being our support structures. Those trips really knitted us tightly because there was no separation between people — there was only a distinction when it was time to work, like during training, and then to relax together with big meals and games nights in the evening or just relaxing by the pool in the afternoons. Some of the staff are away from their partners, kids and the rest of their family for most of the season so to be with everyone for a week was honestly life-changing. Including all of us has created a bond that's unbreakable really.'

The gatherings have not only been used to solidify team spirit, but can be show of defiance, breeding the determination to recover from setbacks. A case in point was the party scheduled after the 2016 Europa League final at the Novotel in Basel. Klopp had decided leading up to the game that regardless of what happened against Sevilla, Liverpool's players and staff would converge to have food, drinks and a dance afterwards. It was even more imperative to do so if the club lost the showpiece, with the manager reasoning that it is easy to illustrate unity as victors, but the true power is being able to do it in the darkest moments.

Sevilla went into the encounter hoping to make it a hat-trick of tournament wins, while the Merseysiders had been stinking out the continent since failing to qualify from a Champions League group featuring Fiorentina, Lyon and Debrecen in 2009–10. Liverpool were painted as favourites for the final, but they were only seven months into the Klopp era and were not as attuned to the stage as their opponents. Having ceded the League Cup final to Manchester City on penalties earlier in the season, they were still learning that the process trumps the scoreline at the start of a development phase. And a huge part of the journey is, to borrow from Klopp, 'not staying on the floor like silly idiots' after a knock.

Liverpool took the lead against Sevilla through a sublime Daniel Sturridge effort, but were comprehensively outplayed in the second half to surrender 3–1. No one was in a mood for a party that night, but their presence was non-negotiable. Achterberg was so distraught that he compromised: he didn't want to be jovial, but hung around long enough to show his face and have a drink before retiring to his suite. The next morning, when he heard tales of what had transpired, he wanted to kick himself for missing it.

In the early hours, Klopp gathered everyone on the dancefloor and grabbed the mic. He scanned the expansive room and noticed how the despondency that coloured the final whistle all the way back to the

Novotel had already partially dissipated. 'Two hours ago you all felt shit,' he said. 'But now hopefully you all feel better. This is just the start for us. We will play in many more finals.'

Klopp then broke into a rendition of '*We are Liverpool, tra-la-la-la-la!*,' which built to a crescendo as everyone joined in. 'I am still so devastated that I was not at the party and that I left,' Achterberg says. 'Everyone spoke about the power of the moment, about how they felt lifted after the speech. Even today, there is talk about how the gaffer showed us that you can be beaten, but you can't be broken. If you are together, you can keep coming back stronger. That is a remarkable characteristic of what he's built here.'

When Liverpool finally got their hands on the league trophy at Anfield on 23 July 2020, it was unsurprising to hear the players credit the environment at Melwood as instrumental to helping them shake off disappointments and continuously deliver.

'What we have is very special,' Van Dijk told the club's media channels. 'Not only the group of players, the whole mentality of Melwood and everyone who is involved from the kitchen to the kitmen — everyone is a part of it. It's all down to the manager, everyone is involved, and I think that's a very incredible environment to be in. It's down to the work we do on the pitch, at the end of the day, because you need to get results. But if everyone around us is on the same page, it makes it a lot easier to go in the direction we all want to go.'

Pep Lijnders believes the impact of the bonds built off the pitch cannot be overstated. 'Melwood is a special place,' he explains. 'But I truly believe that people make a building. The energy, the trust, it's like a small, close family even though it's such a big club. I didn't have one day in the last two years since coming back when the atmosphere was the wrong one. It's where all the points are made.'

Apart from enhancing the mood of the place, Klopp actively sought to ensure Liverpool are leaders in every field off the pitch. 'When I came in I didn't want to change things immediately,' he said. 'I wanted to understand why English football teams, especially Liverpool, do things the way they did. And so we changed it little by little and we brought quality in for sure. That is something I'm very proud of.'

Klopp used his first half-season to assess where major improvements could be made and did a lot of homework in ascertaining the right experts to head two fundamental areas: conditioning and nutrition. In the summer of 2016, the club poached Andreas Kornmayer and Mona Nemmer from Bayern Munich. The latter has completely revolutionised the way Liverpool's players and staff consume, think of, and feel about food.

'She has literally fuelled us into champions,' captain Jordan Henderson says. 'With Mona it's not just about what you eat and when, you learn everything about your intake without being overwhelmed by information. She's made understanding nutrition so simple.'

Nemmer studied the theoretical aspect of nutrition before taking up an apprenticeship as a chef to master the practical side in Germany. When the national team were looking for someone to cater to their youth sides, they turned to her. The requirements were initially quite basic: prepare delicious, healthy meals in the right portions and warn players what to avoid on certain trips. But Nemmer's passion to properly get to grips with the science of food saw her attend conferences, speak at them, spend days buried in research and ultimately take another apprenticeship in sports nutrition.

She had the gift of getting players interested in food, which Bayern profited from at the Allianz Arena for three years. They did not want to lose Nemmer's talents, but Liverpool's offer was too good to ignore: she would become the head of nutrition, designing the department as she saw fit with full support from Klopp and Fenway Sports Group. She felt the club were as serious about sourcing local, seasonal produce and making small, but meaningful changes down to what kind of salt was being used.

The canteen at Melwood before and after her arrival 'feels like a different world', according to McNally. 'Since Mona came in, the whole kitchen set-up got completely overhauled,' she says. 'So much thought went into the food, the juices and everything people were consuming. You go in and she's made it like this cool, delicious health shop. There's so much choice of everything – whether it's salad or milk – and there are all these boards about nutritional benefits. It's not only the players who appreciate it and learn, the staff do too. She's made a big difference to the diets of everyone at Melwood and always brightens up the place with her personality. Jürgen has such a great eye for people who are brilliant at what they do, but also fit in so well.'

Kornmayer, who the manager calls the 'drill sergeant', arrived to head up fitness and conditioning, having been held in the highest esteem by Bayern's squad. 'He's an absolute mastermind in all the things he has to do for us,' Klopp said. 'Korny is an experienced guy who has worked together with the best teachers and the best players. Education and experience are the most important things in this job and he combines these two things in the perfect way. He fits together perfectly in our coaching team. I think the players will feel the benefit. Athletic fitness, it's not a case of "do it today, feel it tomorrow", it's all about doing the right things and then repeating them to reach the next level.'

There were further big additions too. Lee Nobes spent 11 years with Manchester City before being pinched to serve as Liverpool's chief physio in November 2018. Vitor Matos left Porto, where he was assistant coach of their B team, to become head of the club's elite development in October 2019 and is seen as 'the guardian of the future generation'.

Philipp Jacobsen, from the famed Aspetar, the Qatar-based orthopaedic and sports medicine hospital, took up the newly created position of medical rehabilitation and performance manager, while Thomas Gronnemark acts as a consultant to minimise errors from and maximise the use of throw-ins. Jack Robinson began working as first-team assistant goalkeeping coach in September 2018, while fitness coach Conall Murtagh was promoted from the academy to round up some of the main changes at the training complex. Chris Morgan, who was employed at the club for a decade and served as Steven Gerrard's personal physio, was brought back into the fold after he was let go in 2016, when he had a spell at Crystal Palace before being poached by Arsenal.

'I cannot perform miracles and I cannot find the best

people for the job just by passing them on the street,' Klopp says. 'So what I try to do, is to be up to date all the time, try to understand what other people at other clubs are doing. And if there's something I want to bring in which we didn't have, let's try. Then you have to come together and show respect to their knowledge and they show respect to the process. My blessing in life is that most of the jobs — except Mona's — I already did when I became a coach.

'I was my own analyst. I studied sport science, so fitness and conditioning is not completely new to me. I did pretty much everything in my first few years. So I know how hard all of it is and that's why it's easy for me to respect what they do. That's not only with my coaching staff, but for everyone. I love having a good relationship with LFCTV too, for example. When we meet, why shouldn't we have a good time? This is my thinking not just about sports, but about society and life.'

That explains a headline outgoing too. Klopp's long-term assistant Zeljko Buvac departed the club in April 2018 after a falling out with a number of staff. The Bosnian–Serb's cold personality increasingly jarred with the warmth around Melwood and his brash dealings with colleagues were getting harder to stomach — as evidenced when he publicly lashed out at Achterberg for Liverpool not readying Adam Lallana to come on quickly enough against Chelsea in November 2017. Willian equalised shortly after the substitution was due to be made at Anfield and Buvac held that against the goalkeeping coach for a long time, even though the delay was due to tactical instructions about changing the system.

He clashed with Lijnders too, being neither a fan of his optimism nor enthusiastic about his growing influence on training sessions. This prompted the Dutchman to leave for six months, where he was at the helm of NEC Nijmegen. When Buvac exited in April 2018, it was only a matter of time before Lijnders returned to Merseyside, and this time in a more prominent role.

Klopp's relationship with his former assistant Buvac spanned nearly three decades — from teammates in Mainz to a partnership in the dugout — but a breakdown had been slowly building since their time at Borussia Dortmund. Staff at the German side also found Buvac to be draining, petulant and someone who saw himself as a manager rather than a No 2, which bred some resentment. He was a 'football bible' but could also be antagonistic.

In order to protect the professional and personal bonds that had been so wonderfully crafted at Melwood, Klopp decided it would be in Liverpool's best interests if their spell working together ended. He would have found a different solution if he thought

Buvac's departure would have a negative impact on the squad or staff, but in the event the strength of the team behind the team was only further solidified.

Klopp has taken great pride in overseeing a 'world-class team on the pitch, a world-class team off the pitch, all working in a world-class environment'. Klopp's gigantic personality can often disguise his lack of ego as a manager. Those who work with him, however, single out his trait of never thinking he is always right and his willingness to amend his stance. 'You feel that he trusts people 100 per cent in their job,' McNally says. 'He's also the type of person that will admit, "I don't know everything. I don't know that side of the game." And so he doesn't micro-manage, he lets every department get on with things. People thrive in that situation, as we've all seen. The standards are so high at Melwood, Jürgen is so demanding and yet everyone walks into the building happy to come to work and give their all for Liverpool. He has achieved that balance by really caring about his people, while also always showing his gratitude for all the effort.'

Achterberg highlights that, while Klopp affords staff responsibility for their speciality areas, he is stern when changes are need to be made. 'The gaffer never shies away from a big decision,' he says. 'Never. If something is not right or doesn't work or he's not happy about how it's being done, he will tell who needs to know.

But he doesn't only find problems, he always offers solutions.'

Aside from elevating the football operation at the training ground, Klopp has had a sizeable impact on advancing infrastructure at Liverpool and growing revenue streams. When FSG hired the German, they were certain he could holistically upgrade the club as he had done so at Mainz and Dortmund. He did not only count flipping a finger to the odds, playing superb football and collecting silverware as success. For Klopp, the true measure of any manager is how much you can still feel their influence long after they've gone.

The construction of the new Main Stand at Anfield was completed under his watch and the 53-year-old pushed for the development of one base to house the first-team squad and Liverpool's academy. During his opening week on the job, Klopp would travel to Kirkby to watch the club's talented youngsters, but travelling between both sites regularly was not feasible. While Melwood is historic and became a home away from home for the German, he believed a new state-of-the-art training facility would be hugely beneficial. FSG agreed and sanctioned the £50 million build of a 9,200 sqm HQ in Kirkby, due to open ahead of the 2020–21 campaign despite a coronavirus-enforced delay.

The designs for the complex were inspired by Red

Bull Salzburg's pioneering academy, with Klopp involved in the planning along with sporting director Michael Edwards and Alex Inglethorpe, manager of the club's youth setup. The open-plan recovery rooms, hydrotherapy area, large indoor sports hall and specialist sports rehabilitation suites mirror the innovation from the Austrian club.

Even the work around redeveloping the Anfield Road End has Klopp's fingerprints on it, and when it comes to how finances have been bolstered since his appointment, there has been a 113 per cent increase in broadcasting revenue, 62 per cent in commercial and 43 per cent from matchday income. He has made Liverpool hugely successful on the pitch and has laid foundations for long-term progress with better infrastructure, all the while operating within the confines of a sustainable model that does not rely on massive owner investment.

Klopp gets involved in the little details, too. When Liverpool were designing a new team bus that is regarded as the benchmark in England in terms of facilities, boasting reclining seats and a full kitchen, the manager was part of discussions from start to finish. He even selected the words on the wrapping of the coach, with 'We are Liverpool' across each side, the club crest taking pride of place at the front and 'You'll Never Walk Alone' across the rear window.

'He cares so much about this football club, about the players, about the staff, about the fans and you see it every day over and over again,' McNally says. 'Jürgen gives all that he has to making sure Liverpool is the very best it can be in whatever way and that's noticeable wherever you look.'

After the club lifted the Premier League trophy, the in-house media team wanted to pull together a Champions documentary featuring some of the core staff at Melwood. Klopp was so happy that they would be getting a deserved platform to speak about their contributions that he rearranged training schedules to afford everyone the opportunity to be interviewed at length. He was emotional while watching the footage because, as he continuously emphasises, nothing could have been achieved without the effort, the sacrifices and the resolve of the collective.

Klopp is not a one-man show and he never has been. The wall outside his office may act as a symbolic reminder of that, but the evidence is scattered all through Liverpool's success. They have become the best team on the pitch because they are powered by the best team off it.

6

Reawakening the Fanbase

'From day one, he [the manager] drew a picture for the fans of how they could help turn Liverpool into a force.'   *Adam Lallana*

'How is this possible?' Jürgen Klopp enquired. 'How can they keep up this level of noise consistently? How is there just a sea of passionate people, a sea of red? How is there so much meaning in their eyes. You can never imagine this because you don't think this is possible.'

As Liverpool's open-top bus approached the Pier Head by the Mersey waterfront, showered in confetti and surrounded by supporters as far as the eye could see, the manager was a cocktail of emotions: proudly sporting his Liverpool black cap, tears wet his trademark clear glasses as he cracked the widest smiles.

He laughed wildly, pausing intermittently, puffing out his cheeks in disbelief. Liverpool were parading their sixth European Cup — the first trophy of the Klopp era — around the city, with 750,000 people congregating on the way from Allerton Maze to the Albert Dock, where fireworks set off from the water to illuminate the sky, and the German could no longer hear anything other than the sound of the players' hands banging on the bus as they joined in the chorusing of the fans' favourite songs.

For the three quarters of a million people that lined the streets, however, Klopp was the voice inside their heads. How was this possible? He made it so. The city of red on that Sunday 2 June 2019; the sight of Madrid's Plaza Felipe II square a day earlier being carpeted by close to 60,000 fans ahead of the 2–0 Champions League final victory over Tottenham; the unthinkable comeback over Barcelona in the previous round; the intoxication of Shevchenko Park a year earlier in Kiev; that unbelievable night against Borussia Dortmund at Anfield in 2016. You'd have to transport yourself back to the manager's first month in charge, November 2015, to understand the true meaning behind those scenes.

Right from the beginning of his Liverpool tenure in 2015, Klopp spoke directly and powerfully to Liverpool fans when he needed to. On 8 November, he suffered his first defeat, when Scott Dann headed Crystal Palace 2–1 up in the closing stages at Anfield. The goal promoted home fans to exit Anfield en masse. 'Eighty-two minutes – game over,' Klopp said at the time. 'I turned around and I felt pretty alone at this moment. We have to decide when it is over.'

Neil Atkinson, host of fan channel *The Anfield Wrap*, believes the messaging connected with the fanbase due to the way it was delivered and the fact the manager was including supporters in the process of forcing late goals. 'What Jürgen did really well in the aftermath of that game was he spoke quite emotionally,' Atkinson says.

'He spoke personally about how he felt really alone in that moment. And I've always thought it's a really interesting sort of use of language, you know, the idea that he's stood and he's so bereft of the people around him. And I think that what he sort of got right, and has got right quite repeatedly, is knowing when to appeal to Liverpool supporters practically, and also know when to appeal to Liverpool supporters on an emotional level. That was a really sort of powerful, emotional one.'

Klopp communicates through actions too. Having implored fans to help players believe they can still react in the dying stages of matches, he duly thanked them when his words were enacted. A month on from the setback against Palace, a deflected Divock Origi strike on 90 minutes against West Bromwich Albion secured a 2–2 draw for Liverpool at Anfield. That scoreline against such opposition would not usually prompt fist-pumps and the manager assembling his players at full-time, hands interlinked, to salute the Kop. At the time it was an action extensively derided, with Klopp accused of celebrating mediocrity. What he was doing, however, was thanking the crowd for listening to him. 'I really wanted from the first day that the people know about their importance,' Klopp explained. 'In football, people always say it — that supporters are important — but then you don't treat them like that so you have to make sure it's a really healthy relationship.

'We know without them we wouldn't play on our highest level, no chance. You have to appreciate that and it's very easy for me, but it's still very different routines in England and in Germany.

'There was a big misunderstanding against West Brom. I wanted to say thank you to the supporters after that game so I took my team towards the Kop to do it and there was a discussion everywhere about it. For me, it was "why should we even discuss that?" But I had to learn that English people are not used to that kind of thing. I wanted to show that we really are one unit, 100 per cent one unit. That means I know I am responsible for the performance, but the people are responsible for the atmosphere.

'So it should be a win-win situation. When we play well, it's easy to get the crowd going and when we don't play well, we need you to encourage us — get on your feet, tell us "come on" — you have to be the stars then. I want us to have the best atmosphere in world football and there is no limit to what we can do actually.'

Klopp would later admit taking the fans to task so soon was quite bold. 'When I said I was pretty alone against Crystal Palace, I think that was a brave phrase,' he said in LFCTV's *Golden Sky* documentary. 'If people don't like you, they could say, "What do you want? Get the team to play some good football and stop criticising us." The LFC supporters instead though say, "Maybe he's right, let's try." That led to the West Brom moment which the outside world misinterpreted but it was a thank you to the fans for being with us. It feels 100 per cent like home now. It's all about the people, that's why it was so important to get this connection back.

'It's not about noise, most stadiums in the world are noisy. It's about understanding, it's about involvement. If I close my eyes, I can tell pretty much everything that is happening in the game thanks to our crowd. It's so supportive in the right way. They really throw their soul onto the pitch.'

Adam Lallana, who assisted Jordan Henderson for the opening goal against West Brom, remembers thinking of that thank you to the Kop after the parade. 'The gaffer's ability to pick up on things so quickly, to address it while we all only realise much later what his objective was is unreal,' the midfielder says. 'From day one, he drew a picture for the fans of how they could help turn Liverpool into a force, and if you count all the amazing experiences created together since then, it just shows you how intelligent he is not just in a foot-ball sense, but with people.'

As much as Lallana was awed by the way Klopp commanded the supporters, they were captivated by his authority with the players. 'We all went on this journey with Jürgen,' he says. 'The squad listened to him, the fans listened to him, as well as the staff and the owners. I will always be blown away by how power-fully he got the supporters onside. He was never scared to address anything with them when most managers would rather avoid kicking up a fuss cos they don't want to become unpopular.'

Klopp's talent of being true to himself is the trait Neil Atkinson believes resonated most with those affil-iated to the club. 'I think what the crowd warm to isn't just simply the idea that he's in some way, shape or form one of us, but it's as much the notion that he is simply one of him — he is authentic,' the award-winning podcaster explains.

'I think people like the fact that he's clever without wearing it heavily. I think they like the idea that he's engaged in political and social issues, but without endlessly banging on about them. I think that they like the fact that he comes over as though he is well rounded, but I think more than anything else, people like the fact that he manages to simultaneously be larger than life, but also be genuinely authentic to his own essence.

'The most striking thing about him is how much he is committed to who he is and that isn't always a gregarious thing; it's not all hugs, it's not all everything's absolutely marvellous. There's a real engagement with what's in front of him.'

One instance was the furore in February 2016 over £77 tickets being announced for a section of seats in the Main Stand. Club legend Jamie Carragher pointed out the cost was 'too much to watch a game anywhere' but that it was 'particularly over the top in Liverpool'. The Spion Kop 1906 group, backed by Spirit of Shankly, suggested a walkout on 77 minutes during the home match against Sunderland in protest. The team were 2–0 up when thousands left their seats at Anfield on 6 February, with Sunderland scoring twice shortly afterwards. Klopp had missed the fixture following an operation to remove his appendix, but when the ticket fiasco was put to him, he declined to side with the owners. 'It's not what we want,' he said. 'What I know is everyone in the club has a big interest in finding a solution. We don't want people to leave the stadium before the game is finished.' FSG scrapped the pricing, introduced more fan-friendly cost measures like ending game categorisation so supporters part with the same money for matchday tickets regardless of the opposition, and apologised for the 'distress caused'.

Klopp pushing for a solution rather than blindly backing FSG was a huge deal given how impassioned the fanbase — especially locally — was about Liverpool leading the way for fairer fees as opposed to hitting them with extortionate prices. 'He doesn't take the side of the ownership over the £77 tickets and the walkouts, so supporters know he's willing to help the cause,' says Atkinson. 'He's not simply agreeing with the people who pay him and that aids the process of trust and becomes part of the feeling that we're all heading in same and the right direction. Klopp has changed the mood music around Liverpool Football Club, who are a lot more open to being representative, to enjoying themselves, to helping the supporters enjoy themselves. He's actually flagged the support as a positive, rather than as a problem to solve. You compare that now, to the atmosphere after the walkout, and it is markedly different.'

While Klopp had to make some 'big balls' moves in his opening period at the helm, Liverpool showed their cojones on the pitch. 'We produced some incredible performances and results that stood out,' Lallana says. 'You could see the fans feeding off the aggressive way we were playing, suffocating opponents, and we were also reacting to their energy. Our Europa League run was very special, the domestic games away to Manchester City and Chelsea early on also set a marker. There were signs that everything was slowly coming together.'

When Klopp outlined his blueprint to FSG for four hours in New York in October 2015, restoring Liverpool as a continental powerhouse was a central theme. The club did not make sense without European football and the fanbase needed their tradition of turning public squares all over the mainland into a scarf-swirling, banner-draped haven. Five months later, fierce foes Manchester United were comfortably dispatched with an aggregate score of 3–1 in the Europa League round of 16. The quarter-finals against tournament favourites and Klopp's former side Borussia Dortmund was when the realisation of what Liverpool were capable of finally landed. The Merseysiders had returned from the Westfalenstadion with a 1–1 draw, but found themselves 2–0 down at half-time in the second leg at Anfield.

BVB were a counter-attacking marvel, a fusion of slick transitions and highly technical footballers, but they capitulated 4–3 under the 'emotion and passion' at the historic ground. Their manager at the time, Thomas Tuchel, stood speechless as goals from Philippe Coutinho, Mamadou Sakho and Dejan Lovren contributed to another ridiculous night under the Anfield lights. 'If you expect an explanation, I have to disappoint you,' he said. 'It was not logical. If you have such a strong belief then things can happen.' Neil Atkinson agreed that Dortmund was a 'really strong reminder to the fanbase of how we influenced this kind of magic in the past and how we can influence it in the present and future'.

Jamie Webster, an electrician by trade who is now a full-time musician after headlining the BOSS Night gigs and being promoted and included in events by Liverpool, could sense fan culture — songs, flags, merchandise, clothing — being revived upon Klopp's appointment, but the displays in the Europa League were crucial building blocks for the stunning reawakening to come.

'Supporters were thirsty for attacking football with fight, to see players leave it all the pitch again,' Webster says. 'The early performances, especially in Europe against United and Dortmund, were very Jürgen Klopp and very Liverpool, so you could see these two strong parts coming together so well and that was livening up the stands. There were teams better than Liverpool on paper, but we were braver and the supporters really bought into that. Even though we lost the final against Sevilla in Basel, there was enough proof to see he was building Liverpool into a team the opposition really feared again and turning Anfield into a fortress.'

Neil Atkinson reasons that Klopp's enterprising style of play corresponded with the club's supporters deciding they had enough of misery and were ready to commit to having a good time. 'While it's the majority of what the manager has done that has galvanised the fans, there's a little element of it being built upon Liverpool fans choosing to enjoy themselves more. You can see that in all the stuff around, for instance, the BOSS Nights, the live *Anfield Wrap* events and such. There's been a feeling to get more out of following this club, to get as much out of it as humanly possible. Klopp carries this over as he has the same values. He wants us to have the best time, but he also wants to get the most out of his resources. That underpins so much of this, the idea that this is meant to be fun.'

The above could only materialise with regular Champions League football. The aim for Klopp's first full season at Liverpool was a top-four finish, an objective that would go down to the final game of the 2016–17 campaign with Middlesbrough the visitors to Anfield. Gini Wijnaldum scored just before half-time, receiving Roberto Firmino's pass and hammering the ball beyond Brad Guzan and high into the goal in front of the Kop. The relief and release around the stadium was staggering after a goal that provided the platform for a 3–0 victory. 'It was tense,' Wijnaldum recalled. 'You could also see, I think, that because we didn't score that early the fans were a little bit nervous. I think even we as players were a little bit nervous because you know that you're playing at home, you know that you have to win.

'When we scored the goal it looked like things just fell off our shoulders and we didn't have the heavy weight anymore. There was already pressure before we went into that game and the longer the game went without us scoring a goal, the more the pressure was going up and up and up and finally there was the moment.'

Sealing their place in the Champions League play-off reinvigorated the players, the supporters and Klopp. 'Usually at the end of the season you are tired but I am already looking forward to it,' the manager said. 'It is the best tournament in Europe. There is nothing better maybe in the world. You want to be there. Liverpool needs to be there consistently. We will be really strong and really fight for it and we want to be there. In the last ten years Liverpool was not a part of it too often.'

The club's return to Europe's premier tournament, knocking Hoffenheim out to enter the competition proper, was the real catalyst for fan culture beginning to fly. 'It felt like a rebirth of Liverpool, not just on the pitch, but on the terraces,' Webster says.

In February 2018, when the Reds rocketed Porto 5–0 in the Champions League last 16 at the Estádio do Dragão, the supporters' song 'Allez, Allez, Allez' first got its airing on concourses. Webster heard the words of the song and decided to enhance the melody. He sped it up a little and altered the rhythm of the clap. That chant was lift off for the fanbase and changed his life.

> '*We've conquered all of Europe,*
> '*We're never gonna stop,*
> '*From Paris down to Turkey,*
> '*We've won the f***ing lot,*
> '*Bob Paisley and Bill Shankly,*
> '*The fields of Anfield Road,*
> '*We are loyal supporters,*
> '*And we come from Liverpool,*
> '*Allez, allez, allez.*'

'That song has taken me around the world and put me in such unbelievable situations for the last two years

— playing it with Alisson, playing it for Klopp and then even having beers with the gaffer,' Webster says. 'Things that I thought would never happen to me just became so normal because the players and manager made it feel that way.'

The singer-songwriter, whose debut album 'We Get By' was released in August 2020, has soundtracked many of the game-changing fan experiences of the last few years. 'The only way I could top it, is if I was playing for Jürgen in his starting eleven,' the Scouser says. 'That's the only way I could have a better job right now. I'm representing Liverpool the city and our people when I go on tour and sharing our culture, which is massively important. The club — as an institution, as a business — means so much to millions around the world, but it's crucial to protect its identity, where it all started, its home. The very essence of the city, of Scousers, of how the club came to be what it is, should be at the forefront along with the football. I can't explain how much it means for me to be helping with that. Fair play to the club for promoting fan culture and to BOSS Nights who have built the experience from the ground up. There used to be 50 to 60 people turning up in 2012–13, now we're sold out at massive venues and travelling with the club putting on unforgettable fan parks. Liverpool have really embraced what is going on here through Klopp reaching out to

The Anfield Wrap, Redmen TV, BOSS Night . . . How the club is run with him as manager is exactly how it should be: where everyone feels part of the whole.'

Liverpool followed up the scorching of Porto with a 5–1 aggregate humiliation of Manchester City in the quarter-finals. Everything felt possible and nothing seemed beyond the group. Roma were then dispatched 7–6 on aggregate, the team having nothing to lose that night at the Stadio Olympico following a 5-2 first-leg hiding of the Italians at Anfield. In Italy, the bond between the players and supporters was evident. After the final whistle, the squad held up a banner for Liverpool fan Sean Cox, who was assaulted outside the ground in the first leg and put in a coma.

Sadio Mane broke the security barrier to get closer to the crowd, while Trent Alexander-Arnold and Ben Woodburn came back out from the dressing room to celebrate with the fans and Liverpool reaching the final. Klopp also returned to spend an extended period saluting the supporters. In Kiev, the host city of the Champions League final against Real Madrid, fan culture was ratcheted up another notch. Despite flights and accommodation being close to impossible and ridiculously expensive to secure, the Ukraine was flooded with Liverpool faithful.

The stories behind some of the trips were both touching and underscored how much being back at the pinnacle meant. Sean Quinn, for example, surprised his father Billy in Kiev after travelling for three days from Australia, passing through six different airports. The week after overcoming Roma, Liverpool's head of tourism Tom Cassidy began sketching a fan event. Having liaised with Webster, BOSS Night, *The Anfield Wrap* and Redmen TV, his plans came together in 10 days. Shevchenko Park would be the spot for supporters to converge on the afternoon of matchday and despite the sound system not being powerful enough or the stage big enough, there was a surreal happiness that blanketed the place.

Tens of thousands — friends, families, strangers — all swayed, bounced, raised their fists and their pints while amplifying their voices in celebration of the football club. 'The sense of togetherness we had at Shevchenko Park made everything worthwhile,' Webster remembers. 'It was pure joy. If you could bottle that, it would be priceless. We walked to the ground feeling invincible. We celebrated before the game probably better than we could have done had we won the game. I still can't really find the words to describe the euphoria and pride that afternoon gave to us. The park was incredible, the concourse was nuts and then Dua Lipa played "One Kiss" as part of the pre-match entertainment and everything went off . . . only Scousers!'

Chelcee Grimes, a singer-songwriter from Liverpool

and fan of the club, takes up the story. 'I worked with Calvin Harris in Los Angeles around six months before the final and after Kiev, I was in the studio with Dua working on writing "Love Again" which is on her new album, which was a bit mad to have done stuff with both of them with this massive game sandwiched in-between,' she says. 'I showed Dua the videos of the Liverpool fans going crazy in the stands and she was in disbelief as to how "One Kiss" had just taken over. Ben Mawson, one of the owners of TaP Management, our talent company, is a big Liverpool fan and he was so made up about it all. It was really cool and it was just so us.'

Klopp's charges lost the final 3–1 to Real in cruel circumstances, with Salah's injury and Karius' horrible errors, but the overriding mood departing the NSC Olimpiyskiy Stadium was one of defiance. Those who were at Shevchenko Park were certain something special was brewing.

'It was the start for this team. That's what it felt like,' says Atkinson. 'They would all be ready to spark off one another again and go and achieve everything that they wanted to achieve. But the reason why was because not one of them was thinking, "I can achieve this better somewhere else" at that stage. And I think that that has always been the most important thing, that Klopp has got the right players, done the right things with them and he's kept them. Rafa Benitez, for example, wasn't able to deliver that. There was still a big chance of Steven Gerrard going after the Miracle of Istanbul and the idea that he would always have to sell to buy. Klopp had a great base, needed to add to it and Liverpool would be back. You couldn't doubt it.'

In 2018–19, Liverpool would hurdle Paris Saint-Germain, Napoli, Red Star Belgrade, Bayern Munich, Porto and Barcelona to reach a consecutive Champions League final. Before they beat Mauricio Pochettino's Tottenham 2-0 at the Wanda Metropolitano, they showcased a European masterclass against the Bundesliga giants and decimated Leo Messi and co in a historic comeback. It was the perfect combination of belief from the stands and the squad that they could deliver the impossible.

'We know this club is the mix of atmosphere, emotion, desire and football quality,' Klopp said in the aftermath of a barely believable night. 'Cut off one and it doesn't work — we know that. I've said it before. If I have to describe this club then it's a big heart and tonight it was obviously like crazy, pounding like crazy. You could hear it and probably feel it all over the world. I'm so happy we could give the people this experience and I'm really happy about having another chance to get things right from our point of view.'

The club were at another European final, with another

pre-match party in store. In the northeast tip of Madrid, the Plaza Felipe II square was remodelled into Liverpool heaven. Around 60,000 fans squeezed in to experience collective exhilaration. In the build-up to big night games, having an afternoon snooze is a typical part of Virgil van Dijk's preparation routine. Having seen videos of the Liverpool supporters celebrating with all they had, the pedigreed centre-back chose to stay awake and consume as much of the content as possible to fuel him for the final. 'Normally I get a little sleep before a match, but it was difficult,' he said. 'It makes you happy even before the game to see all those fans in the square. I was like, ready to go, ready to see my family, see all the supporters and to come out for the warm-up, it was a special feeling. In the end to lift the trophy was incredible.'

'The day in Madrid was the best day of my life,' says Webster, who was the headline act and also performed at the players' party at the Eurostars Hotel that night. 'You dream of those sights, of so many people, of such an occasion. There's so many documentaries on that day, but yet I still can't really sum up the scale of it. Being on stage at the player's party afterwards, it felt like I was having this really long dream and I was going to wake up back on a building site. Everything was too unreal. Seeing Virgil losing his shit to me singing will never leave my mind. I got a playful slap on the face off Jürgen, my girlfriend got a hug and I mean, these are things you don't even imagine happening because you really can't see how it's possible.'

It was long said that the parade of the Champions League trophy in Liverpool would be topped if the club ended its three-decade wait for league glory, but coronavirus has put the celebrations on hold. Unfortunately, while the majority of supporters respected the fact that a global pandemic in which social distancing is essential is not the right time to congregate en masse, thousands converged at Anfield on the night of 25 June 2020 as Klopp's men were confirmed as champions. That spilled over into another gathering at the Pier Head the next day, which resulted in disorder and the fire brigade attending after a firework was aimed at the Liver Building and caused a small blaze. The club condemned the 'wholly unacceptable behaviour' and reminded 'when it is safe to do so, we will all work together to arrange a victory parade when everyone can come together to celebrate'.

Klopp has completely committed to ensuring supporters get a chance — however long it takes to become possible — to share in the achievement, salute it and be thanked for their part in helping make it happen. 'We will wait and then we will come together with millions of people to celebrate,' he said in a moving interview with *The Anfield Wrap*. 'If anybody thinks, "oh, they're a little bit crazy," I couldn't care less.

'If it will happen, it would have been an absolutely incredible ride with all the things that happened last year [missing out on the title to Manchester City by a point] and before that losing the Champions League final in Kiev. It would be an exceptional celebration. Most people will never, ever forget these tough times. We have more time to find the right moment to enjoy it together. And then we can say, like three or four weeks before, "make sure that you are all ready" and we do it.

'Then we can show again how special we are as a club, and that we don't care what others think about us, if they say that we are a little bit mad or whatever. We just enjoy ourselves and celebrate what we are, who we are and what we've won and that would be my absolute dream. So I really can't wait. I can promise, whatever is in my power, I'll do to make sure that we'll have a proper parade — whenever that will be.'

Klopp's word is his bond. 'The man can do no wrong,' says Webster, who received a video of the manager endorsing his debut album unprompted. 'He is an unbelievable person, who truly cares. There's not a Jürgen Klopp for the camera and a different one away from the camera. He is who he is and he wears his heart on his sleeve. He has a good mentality, a good way of dealing with people and is an example that how you choose to live your life can have such a big effect beyond what your job is. By being himself, he has changed not just this football club, but so many lives. He has changed my life. I could never thank him enough. This fanbase will remember him for all time.'

7

Lose Big To Win Big

'He just knew the bigger picture. He could see it clearly . . . He knew going forward that we were going to get better.'   *Jordan Henderson*

Every so often, Pep Lijnders replays a conversation in his head that sparks a smile and a disbelieving shake of his head. It traces back to the end of April 2018. Liverpool had scorched Roma 5–2 at Anfield in the first leg of the Champions League semi-final and Jürgen Klopp was on the phone shortly afterwards. The manager had called to persuade the Dutchman, then head coach of NEC Nijmegen, to re-join his backroom team and made an unforgettable prediction. 'He told me in the third or fourth sentence when he called me that we would conquer the world together,' Lijnders says. 'I never thought he meant this literally.'

The 37-year-old was particularly struck by the conviction of the words and the clarity with which Klopp spelled it out, detailing the growth of the group and the change in psychology. Liverpool would ultimately achieve success on an unparalleled scale for a British club, becoming the first team to simultaneously be champions of Europe, champions of England and champions of the world.

But a month after Klopp had dialled Lijnders, the Merseysiders were on the canvas in Kiev. Real Madrid had floored them in a weird, wretched Champions League final that was decided by an injury, an unloved player and an apparently concussed one. Half an hour into the fixture, Mohamed Salah was in tears as he walked off the Olimpiyskiy National Sports Complex pitch clutching his left shoulder. Sergio Ramos had locked the Egyptian's arm and rolled him judo-style in a challenge that went unpunished but looked suspiciously filled with intent. Gareth Bale, viewed as an annoyance rather than an asset in Madrid, came off the bench on the hour, and within five minutes, had scored a scintillating overhead kick. The scoreline read 1–1 before that triumph of athleticism and technique. Real scored the opener after goalkeeper Loris Karius inexplicably threw the ball against Karim Benzema and watched in agony as it rolled behind him into the net. Sadio Mane equalised shortly after, but Bale banished any hopes of an upset with that piece of mastery which was followed up with a speculative 30-yard effort that Karius, once again at fault, failed to hold and fumbled into his own net.

The victory marked Real's record thirteenth win in the European Cup, their fourth in five seasons and third on the spin. For Klopp, the writing was vastly different. He had lost six of his seven major finals as manager, with only the DFB-Pokal at Borussia Dortmund in 2012 breaking the trend. The defeat in Kiev was Klopp's hat-trick of failures with Liverpool, and while he initially needed time alone after fulfilling his post-match media duties, it was not related to the result or his unflattering record.

The Reds boss had seen his family and friends inconsolable in the stands and caught a glimpse of Ulla attempting to comfort Karius' devastated mother. Klopp spotted Alex Oxlade-Chamberlain, on crutches, with his head bowed as he cried into his palms. And when he ticked off his press duties and was making his way back to the coaching quarters, Salah walked towards him in such a broken state he was unable to speak. Klopp put his hand on the Egyptian's other shoulder and pulled him in, the pair standing there for a few seconds in haunting silence. Klopp excused himself to have a moment on his own because of how the loss, which had emotionally affected his players and loved ones, hurt him too. The result had not gone Liverpool's way, but the personal sacrifices everyone had made was at the forefront of his mind.

It is in these darkest moments, however, when the German is incredibly skilled at finding and sharing the light. At his Formby home in the early hours of the following morning, flanked by assistant manager Peter Krawietz, Die Toten Hosen lead singer Campino and a German journalist, Klopp led an impromptu chant which was caught on a phone camera.

'We saw the European Cup
'Madrid had all the f***ing luck
'We'll just keep on being cool
'And bring it back to Liverpool!'

The defiance was contagious, with players and staff being uplifted by the fact that Klopp was so confident the club would return to the biggest stage. Supporters, meanwhile, ensured the clip went viral across all social media platforms. While his reaction was welcome, it was in no way surprising.

The man from the Black Forest was moulded by defeat, near misses and disappointment. Jürgen Klopp's father, Norbert, competed against him as if they were the same age at every sporting activity all through childhood. Klopp junior, of course, was no match and had to learn how to use being beaten as motivation and an education to get closer to winning. His attempts at becoming a professional footballer were framed by setbacks before he finally made the grade, aged 23.

As a manager there was an immediate acquaintance with painful outcomes. While at Mainz he twice missed out on promotion to the Bundesliga by the narrowest of margins — a point and then goal difference — but he persisted and lead the club to the top flight for the first time in their history.

Christian Heidel, their former sporting director, recalled Klopp's talent at galvanising everyone in the worst of times. 'Jürgen electrified a whole city,' he said. 'Especially after missing out on promotion because of a missing point and a missing goal. He blew away the depression with his speeches after the last matches.

'After missing out in 2003 he announced in front of 10,000 fans in the city centre, "We will prove that it is possible to get up after such pain." He asked the Mainz fans to come to the first training of the new season. There were 10,000 there when training started again. After the last home game in 2007 and the relegation from the Bundesliga, he took the stadium microphone in his hand. No spectators left the stadium. He told them: "We'll be back, no question!" The crowd started celebrating relegation like we'd won the championship.'

His reshaping of Dortmund into a supremely cool, superlatively good club also contained a degree of misfortune. They missed out on European qualification in 2008–09 on goal difference, lost the 2013 Champions League final late on and ceded the German Cup in the following two seasons. Long before he arrived at Liverpool, Klopp had learned to treat defeats as motivation to come back harder, stronger and more refined.

'You can lose big if you are prepared to win big,' Klopp says. 'So I understand it like this, because my life is like this. I lost a lot, a lot of times and it was always really hard, but I learned the next day, life gives you the chance again so you need to be ready to use it.'

At Liverpool, the squad didn't have to wait long to witness Klopp's refusal to allow a loss to linger and cut through the resilience he wanted to implement. A week after the pivotal squad walk towards the Kop following a 2–2 draw with West Brom in December 2015, a Christmas party for everyone at Melwood had been scheduled at Formby Hall. There was just one problem with having an evening of celebration: Liverpool were bulldozed 3–0 by Watford at Vicarage Road that Sunday afternoon in their most abysmal performance since Klopp's appointment. Surely, the party would be cancelled? Surely, it wouldn't be appropriate to be jovial after they were so ruthlessly banjaxed?

Not under Klopp. Performance analyst Mark Leyland paints the scene of how the manager ensured early on that everyone understood that togetherness isn't exclusive to positivity. 'On the plane back, heads were down, no one was talking, it was miserable,' he remembers. 'The gaffer had already sent a message to the Melwood group along the lines of "whatever we do together we do as well as we can and tonight that means we party", but we were still quite down. So he got up, stood at the front and signalled for everyone to take off their headphones. He said, "Right, this ends here. The sulking ends here. As soon as we get to the party, I want to see you with a drink or food in your hands, dancing and enjoying each other's company. That's the rule, that's the only requirement. I don't want anyone going home before midnight — it's our party. If we can be together in our toughest moments, it will lead to so many happy moments."

'Most managers would have been inclined to cancel it,' says Leyland, 'or not put in energy as to who went and how the night turned out. It's unique. He's unique with how he handles situations. There are loads of football managers who've got great tactical knowledge, really good ideas about football or impressive CVs, but without investing in people on a personal level. Jürgen has the whole package and a lot of what he has you can't teach — it's just him. But he's also worked very hard to be among the best in his field, to find the edges, which complements his natural ability to connect with people.'

While Klopp was well versed in difficulty and reacting in the right way, he had to teach Liverpool that failure was not a conclusion, but an important chapter. He got another opportunity to do so four months into the job as the Reds reached the League Cup final against Manchester City, who were rightly overwhelming favourites. But despite outplaying Liverpool for a large part of the game at Wembley, Manuel Pellegrini's men were forced into a penalty shootout after Philippe Coutinho struck on 83 minutes to cancel out Fernandinho's opener. Willy Caballero, selected ahead of Joe Hart in goal, saved kicks from Lucas, Lallana and Coutinho with City winning 3–1 from the spot.

In his post-match debrief, Klopp spoke powerfully. 'We feel down, but now we have to stand up,' he said. 'Only silly idiots stay on the floor and wait for the next defeat.

'We will strike back. We have felt how it is to lose. It is not the best moment but on Monday morning maybe we can change everything.

'We will go on and we will get better. We will reach for finals. We have to work really hard, carry on and there is light at the end of the tunnel. This is important.'

He was right. Three months later, Liverpool were contesting the climax of the Europa League against Sevilla and, despite suffering another setback, they partied at the Novotel in Basel. Losses were not going to overshadow the big picture.

'The message was we carry on,' Lallana says as he thinks back to the aftermath of that night. 'It feels weird initially, you're not really in the mood to party, but then you understand it. You realise that wallowing isn't going to help move you forward. With finals, you can have the best preparation, you can have the best feeling, but you can't control everything that happens over 90 minutes, but you can control how you react to either winning or losing.'

Captain Jordan Henderson spent the entirety of the game against Sevilla on the bench, having not completely recovered from a knee injury sustained against Dortmund in the quarter-final. As Liverpool attempted to regain control of proceedings after Kévin Gameiro's equaliser and a rapid Jorge Andújar Moreno double had rendered Daniel Sturridge's opener meaningless, Klopp turned to Joe Allen instead of the skipper.

Henderson was in emotional turmoil. Was it hard for him to flip the switch and be in party mode after the disappointment of defeat and not being afforded minutes to try and change the outcome? 'Listen, you're probably talking to the worst person in the world when it comes to defeats,' he says. 'So the gaffer is at one end of the scale and I'm probably all the way down the other end. And that's why I feel that I've learned so much through this journey with him, not only as a player, but as a person: how to process certain things, how to deal with certain situations. I take defeat very, very badly. But the parties and the way he'd react helped us sort of put things into perspective and deal with the present better.

'With the Europa League final, I'd just come back from injury and managed to be fit for the game – not 100 per cent, so I didn't come on. I was obviously devastated that we hadn't won and I was in a pretty dark place having just shaken off injury and then we'd lost. The last thing I wanted to do was be dancing around and celebrating in the hotel. So Jürgen would have probably been looking at me thinking, "What's going on here?" while I suppose at the time I was thinking, "Well, this is different. How can he be like that?"

'Looking back, he just knew the bigger picture. He could see it clearly. He knew that this was going to help us, if anything. It wasn't a negative thing. Yes, we'd lost, but in a short space of time we'd reached two finals and put in some incredible performances against top sides. He knew going forward that we were going to get better, we were going to learn from the mistakes, improve and make finals a habit. That was crystal clear in his head whereas I was thinking, "We've just lost the final."'

'Moments like that are really, really big. He is so intelligent, which people won't really see because they don't know how much he puts into things behind the scenes. He is a genius in terms of how he manages people and how he manages a team. Then his grasp of the details that go into football games, whether on the training field or on the pitch, just blows your mind. His genius is not just on a sporting level. Off the pitch, how he treats people and manages us as humans rather than players has a massive influence. I just feel he sees things differently to everybody else and that's part of what makes him special. He has a unique mentality and that's where I really look up to him and I try to learn as much as I can — as a captain, as a player, as a father and just as a man. He's ridiculously experienced and when he's talking to you, you know it's coming from an informed place and one of care. He's had bad times, he's had good times and it's shaped him but neither changes him. Football is never plain sailing, you know, you'll always go through lows and highs, no matter how good of a team you are. But I always feel with him no matter how low we are or how high we are, he knows how to deal with the situation. That just gives us a better opportunity to steer and be successful.'

There is a unanimous view among players and staff at Liverpool that the club would not have 'conquered the world' without having the shared experiences of crushing disappointment. They no longer feared failure, they were no longer consumed by pressure. They were hardened, they were experienced, they were confident.

They also possessed a manager who could shape their minds to shake off disappointment and return stronger. 'He always knows what to say at the right time,' Henderson says. 'You can't learn that. You can't teach that. It's just natural. He's very emotional on the sidelines during a game, but actually at half-time, that is out the window and he relays his messages very clearly.

'After the game, he doesn't usually speak much because he wants to process everything properly, so he waits until the next day. That's win, draw or lose. It's good because it's removed the adrenaline or emotion. When you watch a match back, it can change your perception and you think it wasn't as bad as initially believed, or it wasn't that great.

'In the meetings we have before or after games, I just feel like no one delivers the messages as well as him. It's really a unique gift combining his charisma, his experiences, his knowledge.

'It's probably even more noticeable after big defeats or when we've lost finals. His reaction was totally different to what you'd ever expect, and it wasn't necessarily to say he wasn't hurting, because of course he was and of course he knew it was disappointing. But I always felt he had the bigger picture in his head and he knew what was going to come. He was confident that those low moments were going to make us closer, better and strong. The way he reacted just gave us so much belief as players.

'In a very good situation, he's also good at keeping a lid on it and not letting the group get carried away. The way he is able to communicate regardless of whatever the scenario is one of his best qualities. And how he dealt with the tough times will stick with me most, because that is not just a football lesson but a life one.'

This explains how and why Liverpool believed they could do the unthinkable in an unforgettable Champions League night against Barcelona on 7 May 2019, when convention insisted they had 'absolutely no chance'. Ernesto Valverde's side were comprehensively dismantled 4–0 at Anfield as the Reds overturned a 3–0 semi-final deficit from the reverse leg. Managing such a major comeback during that stage of the competition against such esteemed opposition was only half of the story. To fully appreciate the extent of the miracle, you need to explore the events surrounding it.

Liverpool had entered the last-four tie with a phenomenal season on the line. Their relentless pursuit of the league title was at a no-margin-for-error juncture as the City juggernaut rolled on. They were enjoying a campaign Klopp admitted he'd 'never seen before' of remarkable resilience and consistency, but the team were in danger of having nothing to show for it.

Pep Guardiola's charges were immovable objects domestically and Liverpool were faced with having to erase a 3–0 disadvantage against the majesty of Leo Messi and co in order to have any joy on the continental stage and a shot at silverware to mark their efforts.

The evening before Liverpool hosted Barça, Manchester City captain Vincent Kompany arrowed a 25-yard pearler into the top corner against Leicester, effectively scuppering Liverpool's chance of edging City to the title. A six-day period that began with the heavy defeat at Camp Nou and ended with that hit from the Belgian centre-back enhanced fears that their season could be reduced to another case of 'almost'. It was a sickening feeling. 'Being honest, we knew there was a very slim chance of anything happening against Barça,' Trent Alexander-Arnold admitted.

After all, Liverpool hadn't just lost the first leg in Spain, but would be without key weaponry for the return leg too. Roberto Firmino suffered a torn groin muscle ahead of that match, with Klopp selecting

Gini Wijnaldum as a false nine because he needed 'an offensive player who is quite good in defending, as well as that could work between the lines'. The Brazilian did get substituted on for a cameo but aggravated the issue which ruled him out of the Anfield encounter.

If being without the club's 'important player, connector, finisher, fighter and first defender', to borrow Klopp's description of Firmino, was not arduous enough, Naby Keita had to be removed on 24 minutes due to an adductor problem. Still, after the game, the manager told Lijnders Liverpool were capable of causing serious damage in the second leg. The 3–0 scoreline was harsh and their display was 'brave, very passionate, very lively and in a lot of moments creative and direct'.

However, as preparations began for the do-or-die encounter, there was another sizeable setback to contend with. Salah had suffered concussion during the 3–2 victory at Newcastle, in a match which also did little to suggest Liverpool could keep a clean sheet against Barça. They would be minus two of their explosive front three, as well as their prime midfielder in transition, at Anfield, all while the rearguard shipped five in two fixtures leading into the game.

Everything that could go wrong was materialising. At Melwood on the morning of the match, any smidgeon of deflation over City's result the night before was outlawed. James Milner demanded that the highlights on TV in the canteen be switched off, while Virgil van Dijk was hyping everyone up about his tussle with former Liverpool man Luis Suarez, following the Uruguayan's theatrics in the first leg. Henderson, meanwhile, reminded the squad that exceeding expectations was their speciality.

That tone of defiance was symbolised by Salah's choice of matchday attire — a black shirt with 'Never Give Up' scrawled across the front in bold, white lettering. Klopp asked supporters to turn Anfield into a 'football party' and they shook off the disappointment to oblige. A haze of red smoke filled the air and the chants were ceaseless. 'The atmosphere was already crazy when we came into the stadium, even though everybody knew the first-leg result and who we were coming up against,' Joel Matip told the club's website. 'But the mood was good and it became better and better. It was just crazy. It was like a whole machine working there together — the players, the fans, everyone.'

It was chaos, but one of Liverpool's heroes was calm. With the strategy to suffocate goalkeeper Marc-André ter Stegen in possession, Divock Origi was selected up top. On matchday, Klopp asked the Belgian what his greatest performance in a Liverpool shirt had been. 'Dortmund away' in the Europa League was the response and the instruction the forward received was to match or better that outing. 'I felt at peace,' Origi recalled. 'I went into the match feeling like we were going to do it.'

Along with a deafening crowd, Klopp's pre-match address promoted that feeling. 'I said, "We have to play without two of the best strikers in the world,"' he noted of his team talk. 'The world outside is saying it is not possible. And let's be honest, it's probably impossible. But because it's you? Because it's you, we have a chance.

'I really believed that. It wasn't about their technical ability as footballers. It was about who they were as human beings and everything they had overcome in life. The only thing that I added was, "If we fail, then let's fail in the most beautiful way."'

In the opening minutes, Liverpool showcased a rabid desire to own the ball, snapping at Barça whenever they were in possession. Within 120 seconds, Andy Robertson got stuck into Messi with Alexander-Arnold feeling the left-back 'got under his skin. He was a little bit affected by it.'

The visitors were not concerned by the early pressure. They were so convinced they would score at Anfield that the club's Twitter account declared 'we're going to get at least one'. Barça were prepared to deal with initial onslaught, happy enough to carve opportunities on the counter. But allowing Liverpool to play to their strengths in front of their emotional home support was not very smart. Barça pointed to it as much afterwards, admitting they got sucked into the opposition's design for the game. Suarez hinted that some of his teammates believed the job was already done at Camp Nou and progression would be a formality.

It took seven minutes for Liverpool to banish that notion with Origi's opener. Henderson grabbed the ball from the net, running back to the centre spot with it under one arm and galvanising the crowd with the other. But there would be more obstacles to hurdle. Robertson picked up at injury and had to be replaced at half-time, while Henderson had spent all of the break on a bike so he could play through the pain of a knee niggle.

An 'angry' Wijnaldum came on for the full-back, which pushed James Milner into the 'Robbo' role and suddenly Barça had more swagger about them. That was until the substitute produced two clinical goals in two minutes, the first from a storming run into the box and shortly afterwards a towering header from a Xherdan Shaqiri cross.

At 3–3 on aggregate, Liverpool had wiped out Barça's cushion and had them on the ropes. Then 'the smartest thing I ever saw football-wise', in Klopp's words, stunned everyone. Alexander-Arnold won a corner on 78 minutes, placed the ball and shaped to deliver the set-piece before Shaqiri requested to take it. The young right-back was prepared to give in to his more senior teammate and began to shift away from the ball, before quickly spotting that Barça had switched off. Origi was in the danger area and alive to the situation, so Alexander-Arnold swivelled back towards the ball sharply.

He directed the corner that the striker instinctively finished while making Barça 'look like youngsters' according to Suarez's analysis. 'I looked at the ref, looked at the linesman,' Alexander-Arnold said. 'I didn't believe it happened, I thought it's too easy to have a goal like that in the semis of the Champions League.' But the scoreline was 4–0 and Liverpool had completed one of the most remarkable and stirring comeback victories in the history of European club competition.

At the final whistle, Klopp gathered his 'absolute f***ing monsters of mentality' and conducted a stirring rendition of 'You'll Never Walk Alone' with the staff and squad in front of the Kop, again inviting memories of the West Brom game. 'Whatever we do, if we don't do it in a brave, big-balls way, then it doesn't work at the highest level,' he said. 'The way we played that day, that was the proof that, "Wow, anything is possible."

'"Each team is beatable on a specific day" is a phrase I used when I joined. We only have to make sure that they face the best us on the day. Having that experience as a football manager, being involved in this game, I don't feel pride a lot of time, but I was really proud of that moment. I really thought, "Wow, that's special."'

The night obliterated the feeling that Liverpool would end a special season empty-handed. The league was City's to lose, but there was a steely belief that European glory would come to Merseyside. While nobody knew what the final had in store, Liverpool were confident that their experience a year earlier would help them handle the occasion and any dramas that unfolded.

On the domestic front, Guardiola's Manchester City put together a staggering run of fourteen successive victories to become English Premier League champions with 98 points — one more than their tireless challengers. Liverpool's total was seven greater than Arsenal's 'Invincibles' and 21 points more than Manchester United's treble-winning class of 1999. It would have been enough to claim the championship in all but three of the previous 119 top-flight campaigns based on three points for a win.

While it was deflating to hit a club-record haul in 2018–19 but not seal the title, Liverpool were not defeatist about it. The players and staff saluted City, appreciating the level the teams competed at and the fight they extracted from each other.

It would have been understandable if the Reds felt a little sorry for themselves or wondered what more they could have possibly done to be champions. But Klopp's conditioning of them against such self-pity meant the players were still swinging rather than struck down by the outcome.

'Congratulations to City, they deserved it,' Virgil van Dijk said on the final day of the season, with Liverpool closing off their league season with a 2–0 triumph over Wolves. 'It was a great title race and I've enjoyed every bit of it. I think we are all going to be a little disappointed because we were so close. To get 97 points, to play football like we have played all season, we have to be very, very proud. I don't care about another opinion, but we work so hard every day to be challenging to be as close as possible. City were just a tiny little bit better than us.

'It doesn't mean it is all over. We take a lot of things with us. We will take this on, and hopefully we can challenge next year and do even better. We have to look on the positive side and remember we are still in Madrid. Hopefully, we can end the season on a high. That's what we are going to try and do.'

Liverpool were unbeaten at Anfield for a second successive top-flight campaign for the first time since 1979–80 and were heading to Spain for a second consecutive crack at the Champions League trophy. There was no elation in the dressing room, however. Klopp walked in and broke the silence. 'I couldn't be prouder of you,' he told the squad, trying to keep it together. 'What you have managed this season is incredible. I am so happy to be your manager, I wouldn't swap this group of mentality giants for anyone. You will be winners because that's what you all are.'

He was right. Liverpool would meet Tottenham in the European Cup final on 1 June 2019. Mauricio Pochettino's team had produced a stunning comeback of their own against Ajax in the semi-finals but were strangers to the enormity of the showpiece. Everything is heightened around the main event of the continental calendar and the experience of Kiev gave Klopp's side the edge at the Wanda Metropolitano.

In sweltering conditions in Spain's capital, Liverpool kicked off for an unexpected start. Just 24 seconds into the greatest match in club football, Moussa Sissoko was adjudged to have handled Sadio Mane's ball in the penalty area that struck his outstretched arm. Liverpool had a penalty that was emphatically dispatched by Salah, the second-fastest goal ever in a Champions League final. The shape of the fixture changed, but the Reds were comfortable throughout, managing the game rather than making things happen. The game remained in the balance until the 87th minute, when Spurs failed to adequately clear a corner and Divock Origi directed the ball into the bottom right corner of the net to add certainty to the fact that Liverpool were going to lift their sixth European Cup.

They had lost big, but now was their time to win the biggest prize possible and their first trophy under

Klopp. 'Every bit that we went through together from day one led to that moment, that result to finally getting over the line,' Lallana says. 'If you lose finals, I mean, what else is there to do? You can sulk, but for what? You've got to a final, which is what you want to achieve — giving yourself the opportunity to win silverware. I think that's really where Klopp's expertise comes in. He helped us to view it like this, to think of the whole process and not listen to all the noise surrounding us. He knew it was only a matter of time before we won, because we were doing a lot of things right to get there and were obviously growing stronger together. He would insist we shouldn't overthink why we're not winning finals and would tell us to just give ourselves more chances at winning and we will. Again, he was right. His full view of development is extraordinary.

'Finals are unpredictable, but you can put faith in your process. I've had a conversation with Pochettino about Madrid and he went through all the things they'd done to be ready. Then they concede a penalty within 60 seconds. How do you handle that? How can you prepare for that? How do Liverpool prepare for Mo [Salah] coming off injured in Kiev. I was coming on after 30 minutes having been out for most of the season. There's no guide to any of it. Getting into finals shows progression — it's about the entire journey rather than only the last scoreline. It is a big deal and a huge psychological factor to get the first win. I've spoken a lot with James Milner and he always talks about how massive the first trophy was for Man City to lead to everything that follows. The belief it generates is priceless.

'Once we won in Madrid, it's no surprise that the league has come, that it's come so quickly and with such a big points distance. It's because we got over that first hurdle psychologically, that trophy burden is gone.'

Pep Lijnders agrees that putting silverware on the board added an instant new air around the team. They knew they were good, a nightmare for the opposition and on the right trajectory, but the trophy made all of that absolutely indisputable. 'It was so important for the group of players and how we prepared for it was also crucial. We kept our football routines but also created a more relaxed atmosphere at the training camp by inviting all the families. It was truly special. Every season you have to earn the right to become confident again. We trained really hard, created a positive environment, a real trust between staff and players. Good projects are based on faith and patience. Since the day I came back to Liverpool, I came to win. That was never in doubt with Jürgen, this squad and the dedication of all the people involved, including the supporters.'

At the foot of the Steinernes Meer mountain landscape, Klopp breaks into the widest smile as he rewinds to all the near misses and underlines the character of steel that Liverpool have shown to stay the course. 'When you win trophies, there's always the question — what came first? Was it the team spirit or was it the success? We had a really good relationship before we were successful because we went through really hard moments together that helped obviously,' he says from a meeting room at the stunning Gut Brandlhof hotel.

'In moments like this, you either go in this direction apart or you come together. We got very close through all the missed chances, because we knew we can solve it if we kept the desire and worked really hard, really doing it together. I love, love, love the reaction of the boys. It's a role model for pretty much everybody in sports. We are an example for how to deal with setbacks, how to go again and how to stay together. This is how I understand football, how I understand life and how I understand my team.'

8

Mentality Monsters

'What I really love is that the boys all come from different backgrounds to create a common story here. They are the best example of how special you can make a situation when you really do it together and for each other.'   *Jürgen Klopp*

Jürgen Klopp is rattling through the names of his players in a tone of amazement. Almost overwhelmed, he pauses, takes a breath, smiles and says, 'You cannot imagine how often Pep Lijnders and I set up the training session together, watch it and then look in each other's eyes and think, "Wow, what was that again?" The boys train like it is the last session of their lives and then they play games with that attitude too. On top of that, they are unbelievable people who fought to be where they are now. They still fight every day to be successful.'

It's true that when you look through the names in the Liverpool squad, the first thing you notice is the contrasting backgrounds of the players, from established internationals and foreign talent from around the globe to those who were told they would never make it; from Premier League second-chancers to unpolished gems given a chance to shine brightly. All with the common bond, as Klopp puts it, that they battled hard to reach the top.

In 2012, everything Naby Keita thought he knew about his footballing ability was cast in doubt. Aged 16, he was dodging cars while scoring goals in makeshift street games in Koleya, an area of Guinea capital's Conakry, before going on to attend professional club trials in France. His parents were terrified to let him leave the country, let alone the continent, but supported the youngster's desire to seek a future for himself abroad.

Keita was not part of an academy structure and had never been exposed to the professional side of football before arriving in Europe. He was out of his depth during trials for FC Lorient among others, with the coaches telling him he lacked the tactical understanding to make it in France. The feedback haunted the teenager, who made an effort to watch and take in the game with a more analytical focus as he moved back and forth between Conakry and Western Europe. He wondered if he would ever make it, but decided he would do whatever it took to try so there would be no regrets. Two years later, after impressive performances in the French lower leagues, he was taken on by Red Bull Salzburg.

In the same year over in Scotland, an unemployed Andy Robertson tweeted 'life at this age is rubbish without no money, #needajob'. After being rejected by his boyhood club Celtic at 15 for being too small and weak, the left-back found himself at amateur side Queen's Park, who only covered his travel expenses. He found employment at Marks & Spencer in Glasgow and did odd-job work in the offices at Hampden Park to earn some cash in-between training and lining up for matches on a Saturday.

When Robertson left school, he was in the first team at Queen's Park but it was not feasible for the defender to continue living by the club's moto *Ludere Causa Ludendi* — to play for the sake of playing. He would need to secure a move to a pro club or give up on football altogether, with thoughts of becoming a PE teacher in his mind. 'I was grateful to my mum and dad because they said, "We will give you this season to try and push on and make that dream a reality, but after that you might have to look at other options", but luckily it all fell into place nicely,' Robertson said, after Dundee United came in for him and rescued his football career.

Virgil van Dijk, meanwhile, was battling a potentially lethal abdominal abscess in 2012. 'I was seriously ill,' the centre-back, then at Groningen in the Dutch Eredivisie, recalled. 'The doctors said it was very, very dangerous. I lost around 15 kilos. I had poison in my system and the abscess almost burst. It was dangerous and I was in hospital for 12 days.' A year later and the 21-year-old was on his way to Celtic.

Over on Merseyside, Jordan Henderson planned to use a Europa League fixture against Anzhi Makhachkala as part of a campaign to prove he deserved to remain at Liverpool. The midfielder had been offered to Fulham in a failed part-exchange for Clint Dempsey the previous summer and did not want a similar fate to follow in the winter window.

Sadio Mane was in the process of transferring from Metz to Red Bull Salzburg for just over £3 million, a fee that was criticised as too much for someone so raw. The Senegal international was already accustomed to making people look silly for underestimating him, having turned up to a trial for the club Generation Foot in Dakar — a near 500-mile journey from his home in Bambali — with torn boots and no football shorts. One of the recruiters, Parmalin Diatta, 'looked at me like I was in the wrong place,' said Mane. 'He asked me, "Are you here for the test?" I said I was. He asked me, "With those boots? Look at them. How can you play in them?" They were bad, really bad — torn and old. Then he said, "And with those shorts? You don't even have proper football shorts?"

'I told him what I came with was the best I had, and I only wanted to play — to show myself. When I got on the pitch, you could see the surprise on his face.

'He came up to me and said, "I'm picking you straightaway. You'll play in my team."'

At the start of 2012, Mohamed Salah was still in Egypt with El Mokawloon, while Hoffenheim's Roberto Firmino was a complete non-entity in Brazil. Fast forward and Gini Wijnaldum was relegated with Newcastle, Thierry Henry went viral when he claimed he didn't know what Alex Oxlade-Chamberlain did at Arsenal or was even good at, and Charlie Adam laid Stoke City's failures on Xherdan Shaqiri, despite him being their creative heartbeat and gamechanger.

As you wade through Liverpool's squad, there is a wealth of tales of resilience. 'That is not a coincidence,' Henderson says. 'The manager knows exactly the kind of footballers he wants to work with and the kind of character they need to have. When him, Michael [Edwards] and the rest of the recruitment team are looking at players, they assess the whole package and not just how good someone is on the pitch.

'It's amazing to take in the stories of our squad. If

you go through each player, they've all had to overcome a lot of obstacles to get to this point. Everyone's story is different, but it's united by the sacrifices, the knocks and persistence. For me to know what my teammates have been through, to work with them every day and know the wonderful people they are and the desire they show and then to win especially the Champions League and Premier League with them — I actually can't put that into words. When we got that first trophy in Madrid, I was so emotional seeing how much it meant to all of them, because I know how much of themselves they give to the club and they have given to football. It was the biggest reward as a captain to see the looks on their faces, to see how they were able to share the achievement with their loved ones. We went through dark times together, stuck through it and that has given the good times so much more meaning.

'I think through our team back to front, with the kids we have too, and the club have done an outstanding job with recruitment and the academy. There is so much hunger in the squad and a focus to improve. The desire to evolve and show how good they are, to show the world how good Liverpool are, is so strong. Players that have come have not only been top footballers, but they've been really, really good people. And I'm so lucky to be part of a team like this, that is so close. And I think that makes a difference on the pitch.

'When the manager came in, he encouraged us to do more things together away from football and that was so smart. When you know someone personally rather than just coming in to training every day and then going home, it tightens the bond. You can still be friends with people in a strictly football environment of course, but the relationship becomes so much more powerful when you take work away and it's personal.

'I think that's one of our great strengths that within this team, there are friendships that extend well beyond the game. We'll never forget these times and we'll be friends regardless of where life takes us. We're all in this for trophies and to win but when you can be part of something this special, that is as important as silverware for me.'

Henderson is right: this is all by design. When Liverpool are convinced about a player through meticulous homework that breaks down — both analytically and in terms of gathering references — how well they handle setbacks and stretches as far as how they interact with non-football staff, Klopp meets them to get a personal feel for who they are and how they'd fit in. The manager explains the process: 'We get as much knowledge about the boys as we can. But the most important sign of their character is actually the way they play football before we work together, because that's what attracts us. That's why we are thinking about them. It's their skills, yes, but very important is the character they show on the pitch. So that and that. So it's really rare that you get to see a completely honest football player on the pitch and then you meet him and think, "What kind of idiot is that?" I can't remember that really happening.

'So, you know a lot before you meet the player, but then you get some vital, final information when you see him. What has the same importance is they get a lot of information about me and our working style. Until that point, most of them only know me from TV and some probably think, "he's okay" and others, '"Oh my god, can you please shut the hell up?"

'That's how it is. And that's why these kinds of talks are so important because we make a real agreement in them. I tell the boys, "We are sitting here together because we want to sign you and you want to join us, which is all great, but from now on, less than 100 per cent is not allowed." I know it's only words, but it is the basis for us. From time to time, I remind the boys about our agreement. The target is to reach your highest point as often as possible individually and we throw it together and then it must be pretty much an explosion. And I really like that. So, on my side, I agree to help them 100 per cent and we share responsibility for their future.

'And the intensity the boys show just in training

all the time — wow! I really don't have the words for how much they give me. We've brought Konstantinos Tsimikas in [from Olympiacos] and he feels like he's standing on a motorway in training with everything coming at him at the highest speed. It is always interesting when you make a new signing and they join training and they think, "Oh my god, what is this? What are they? All machines." It takes time to bring yourself to this level and when you reach it, you surprise yourself and realise you can push even harder.'

Klopp has to remind new recruits that they've been signed for the long-term, because the adjustment period to his demands can be lengthy and taxing. Take the example of Fabinho. Within 48 hours of the final whistle of the 2018 Champions League final which ended in defeat to Real Madrid, Liverpool agreed to sign the Brazilian from AS Monaco in a deal worth an initial £40 million.

It was a big outlay and there were big expectations, which Klopp had to cool down. Fabinho was used to playing in a double pivot in midfield, in a less physically demanding, more technique-driven league. He would not only have to learn how to play the No 6 position on his own in a rapid, relentless division, he would have to do it precisely how the manager wanted to fully serve the system.

Fabinho struggled badly during pre-season and even some analytical specialists had taken to social media to wonder if he was a dud and wouldn't be able to translate his impressive data in England. The defensive midfielder had to wait until October to make his first start for Liverpool and was often left out of the matchday squad despite being fit.

While that may have caused panic at other clubs given Fabinho's fee and just how staggeringly off the pace he was, Klopp kept preaching 'it will come' to the player and the hierarchy. FSG president Mike Gordon and sporting director Edwards had already seen the settling-in examples of Robertson and Oxlade-Chamberlain to trust the process.

In France, Fabinho's lack of minutes prompted persistent links to Paris Saint-Germain. There had never been any motioning from his representative, the super-agent Jorge Mendes, for a move. Instead, the player was determined to do everything possible to command a place in the starting XI. Fabinho undertook a specialist gym programme to increase his fitness and power. The aim was to strengthen his thighs and core without reducing his speed to the ball.

Klopp did not have any major discussions with the progressive destroyer when he was on the fringes — there was no need for it. He knew Fabinho would come good once the tactical requirements became familiar to him and the São Paulo native is now among the best in the world in his position.

Liverpool's analysts pull together a philosophy video at the end of each season, which serves as a reminder of what the team stands for on the pitch. It is also a useful tool for new signings to illustrate the best examples of the tenets of the club's footballing identity. When the player sits down with Klopp, Lijnders, Krawietz or any of the backroom or support staff for tactical direction, the clips provide a comprehensive guide of what Liverpool do in every kind of situation whether it be a high-press or a long throw.

Off the pitch, the dressing room is self-governing. Henderson, Milner and Lallana set the standards, with Van Dijk and Wijnaldum part of the senior players' committee. There are hardly ever incidents of ill-discipline to sort out, with one of the rare occasions being young Harvey Elliott receiving a 14-day ban from the Football Association in October 2019 for an 'abusive and or insulting' social media post relating to Tottenham's Harry Kane. The teenager, still at Fulham when he uploaded the offensive Snapchat video during Liverpool's Champions League triumph over Tottenham, was also fined £350 and had to complete a face-to-face education course.

Henderson scheduled a meeting with Elliott at

Melwood and explained how his conduct and actions were unacceptable and didn't just do a disservice to him, but to the club as well. Klopp does not need to get involved in these kind of matters when he has such a strong group of senior players around.

One of the elements the coaching staff flag about the steel of the team is how everyone stood up and took on extra responsibility when Philippe Coutinho, their 'gold dust', departed for Barcelona in January 2018. 'The Magician', who was adored by his peers, had attempted to get the players to help him change Liverpool's mind about refusing to sell him the previous summer.

Involving his teammates in the saga was the piece of disruption that annoyed Klopp the most. The day after agreeing Coutinho's sale to Barça, the manager rounded up the squad in the dressing room at Melwood. He told the team they'd lost a great player and a friend, but the situation was no more than that. Klopp's over-riding message was for the team not to give anyone on the outside a chance to say the Brazilian's exit had affected their season. That they were too reliant on him, that they were average without him. 'This is us. On we go,' were his closing words.

The signing of Van Dijk with the Coutinho money made that task easier, but there was never a day that Liverpool pined for the little Brazilian. The group wouldn't allow it. They had moved on and moved up.

Too much of the team's play was funnelled through the Brazilian out of habit, but also through his elevation as the club's talisman. Liverpool had become a more collective unit without him, and the funds generated from his transfer were reinvested into creating the best defence in the league with the purchases of Van Dijk, followed by Alisson Becker.

But for all the quality the Reds injected into the squad under Klopp, it is a trio preceding his time on Merseyside that are credited as the architects of the environment of excellence for the players.

'Hendo, Milly and Adam, you cannot ignore their importance for the culture here,' John Achterberg says. 'They have exactly the right attitude if you want to reach the highest level — they live, eat and breathe football and take all the steps to make sure they are doing what is needed on the pitch or off the pitch. When it comes to training, or being in the gym, or helping the kids, or helping the new signings, they are an example to the others. You also have Virg and Gini, who are natural leaders. Sadio is quiet, but when he is on the field, his football talks loud. The whole group move in the same direction, and as a coach, they are a pleasure to work with because they are open to improvement and they don't get comfortable.'

One of the hallmarks of the side is the willingness to do whatever is needed for the benefit of the team.

Whether that has been Milner functioning at left-back for a season to help out, even though it cut against his preferences, or Henderson being used on the opposite side of midfield if needed, Fabinho shifting to centre-back, Wijnaldum being used as a false nine, or any other player having to fill in somewhere, there has been little fuss and maximum effort.

The greatest success of this policy was the remoulding of Alexander-Arnold from a midfielder to a right-back who has grown into one of the very best in the world at the age of 21. The director of Liverpool's academy, Alex Inglethorpe was instrumental to this development along with Neil Critchley, who had been head of the Under-18s. Talks with Klopp and Edwards had revealed the clearest pathway to the first team was on that flank and the pair were convinced Alexander-Arnold had all the attributes to excel in that position. But they needed to enhance his endurance both physically and mentally and so designed gruelling conditions for three months in which the most aggressive attacking players would be made to run at him on repeat in training. He would get shouted at for losing the constant one-on-one battles and hated the sessions, but it worked wonders. It removed petulance from Alexander-Arnold's game when things weren't going his way and heightened his resolve not to let opponents get past him, instead being a weapon for them to worry about.

'Just get on with it,' is one of the ways Henderson describes the attitude of the players. 'We want to do what is needed. We're happy to do it, however uncomfortable it is.' There are flashbacks to when Wijnaldum played in the 3–0 victory over Bournemouth in 2018–19 despite suffering with diarrhoea. He was man of the match and had scored despite only being named in the line-up on the morning of the game after missing training with the illness.

'On Thursday night I had a tablet from the doctor for my knee,' Wijnaldum detailed at the time. 'It was a tablet that could induce stomach pains. I took it and I had a pain and thought it was from the tablet. In the end I was vomiting and everyone was a little bit scared. I didn't train on Friday and I didn't sleep at the hotel either because they thought I might infect other players.

'The manager called me and asked if I could play. I said I was as positive as I can be. In the morning I was still weak and had diarrhoea. The tablets helped a lot but even at half-time I had to run off quickly to get to the toilet. At half-time I thought, "Oh no" but I ran inside and managed to control it!'

The whole episode provided a platform for lengthy laughter among the squad, but it also underlined how far players were willing to go to serve Liverpool and each other.

Vice-captain Milner, a senior pro for 18 years with

stints at clubs like Leeds, Newcastle, Aston Villa and Manchester City, believes the group is the 'most together dressing room' he's ever been involved in. 'Hendo is an incredible captain, you see what he's done, Virgil is obviously a big voice in the dressing-room. Gini, these types of guys . . . You could pull any two names out of a hat to share a dining table or share a room and they'd get on,' he says. 'That is hard to find. I look back at the whole journey and credit has to go to the top for bringing in this manager and signing good players who were also good characters.'

What will resonate most about Liverpool finally landing the title for Milner is 'being together at Formby Hall when it happened. I stood at the back, watching the Chelsea–City game, but also the lads and their reaction when the goals went in, the excitement. Seeing that joy will stick with me for a long time. I've seen what the boys have gone through: the pain; hard work; sweat; rockets from the manager. We've all done it together. To be together when we won it was the most special thing.'

Liverpool's players have not only shown incredible commitment to each other but also to the local community and the areas they originate from. During his brief holiday in-between ending the club's title drought and reporting for pre-season, Klopp finally got the chance to enjoy a documentary that was on his watchlist for ages: *Sadio Mane, Made In Senegal.*

'What a story, what a guy. Not that it is any surprise what he does for his people,' the manager says. In one scene, the speedster is standing on the top tier of a school he has built in his village to the tune of £250,000. Below him, the courtyard is heaving with young and old, many clothed in the Liverpool and Senegal kits he has donated. 'I know you want many things,' Mane tells them. 'But education is the priority for our generation. School comes first.' The next goal? 'You should be in good health before you go to work,' he adds and reveals the construction of the hospital he is building for the area should be finished within months.

Mane has also contributed to water projects in the region and Senegal's president, Macky Sall, has credited him as a symbol of hope and possibilities. No wonder there are banners that hang over homes in his village reading: *'l'enfant de Bambali, le fier de toute une nation'* — the child of Bambali has become the pride of an entire nation.

Meanwhile, if you head northeast across Africa to Nagrig in Egypt, Mohamed Salah is the source of so much life improvement. He donated thousands of tons of food to residents of his hometown Bassioun to help families affected by coronavirus and its economic impact. The Egyptian has made a substantial donation to the area's General Hospital and donated five acres of land to build a sewage treatment plant to ensure a stable source of fresh, clean water.

Egypt's National Cancer Institute (NCI) got a $3 million boost from Salah to help restore its facilities after a terrorist attack occurred near the building. And in February 2020, the United Nations announced him as their first ambassador for Instant Network Schools, a programme that connects refugee and host-country students with opportunities for high-quality online education.

In April, as the global pandemic was at its height in England, it was no shock to learn that Jordan Henderson contacted his fellow Premier League captains to organise a coronavirus fund that will raise millions of pounds for the NHS under the #PlayersTogether initiative. The Liverpool captain and his family do a lot of charity work with zero publicity around it, and he was aggrieved when word got out that he was the driving force behind the top-flight's footballers taking action.

In December 2018, Virgil van Dijk paid for the Owen McVeigh Foundation Christmas party, to which 120 children were invited instead of the usual number of 50 courtesy of his generous donation. Liverpool's full-backs Trent Alexander-Arnold and Andy Robertson are key advocates of and suppliers to foodbanks locally — and in the case of the latter, in Glasgow as well.

The Scouser acts as an ambassador for An Hour for Others, and spent Christmas of 2018 handing out presents he bought to 60 families from underprivileged backgrounds, who also had their meals paid for by the youngster.

Meanwhile, Oxlade Chamberlain and Perrie Edwards, his superstar girlfriend from Little Mix, were armed with gifts to supply to kids at KIND in Toxteth.

Goalkeeper Alisson and his wife, Dr Natalia Loewe Becker, are goodwill ambassadors for the World Health Organisation. James Milner has his long-standing foundation, which has been a godsend to the National Society for the Prevention of Cruelty to Children, among other institutions.

'There is so much happening out there, which tells the story of the kind of people in the squad, but it's not even the half of it,' Adam Lallana says. 'There is a lot that never gets written or seen or heard of and I can only say what a pleasure it is to call these lads teammates and friends. It's the perfect dressing room. There's no stereotypical big player or anyone even close to that in attitude. There's no chips on shoulders or no one thinking they've made it or are some kind of super-star. Fair play to Jürgen and Michael and everyone who has put this team together because, honestly, it's just nowhere to be seen. You look at the kids coming through and they're just going to be moulded to not have any of those unhelpful qualities either. They're showing up to the training ground every day, working alongside the champions, this really unbelievable team, who are completely down to earth and are constantly looking to improve. There's no one who thinks they're too good to speak to the groundsmen or the janitor or the dinner ladies. Everyone interacts with each other in the building and takes a real interest in the staff and it's so good for the kids to see that example. It's so big for the culture around the place and I don't think it would have been possible to come up with a better dressing room. You have such different backgrounds, but everyone is just a top bloke and also wants to put in the work, wants to run, wants to cover you . . . And it's a dressing room that takes responsibility. We hold our hands up when we mess up and then do everything to put it right. This group is such a powerful force for Liverpool and I can really see them dominating for the next few years.

'I won't be at the club anymore but I am confident that there won't be any drop off,' Lallana adds. 'Not at all. I fully expect them to keep going. Having worked very, very closely with the young boys over the last couple years, there are three or four of them that are going to be top players. They might not get much minutes next year, but you've seen the potential already with Neco [Williams], Curtis [Jones] and Harvey

[Elliott]. They're training with the best players in the world, with the best attitudes in the world. They're going to absorb the same mentality as the lads. It's such a great place to learn at if you're a young man, because you see how hard Sadio works, you see him in the gym pushing his limits every day. Bobby [Firmino] may do no-look passes and goals, but you then get to see how much effort he puts into being able to do that alongside all the tireless stuff he does.

'It's really amazing. I'm not worried at all about Liverpool keeping this up. Jordan, Milly, Robbo, Virg . . . they won't let standards drop. Jürgen didn't use the "mentality monsters" label lightly, he knows what he is talking about.'

Pep Lijnders nods in agreement. 'The passion, ambition and work ethic of the players made everything happen,' he says. 'Their personality, their drive to win. Our core group take the new players, and the young talents with them — inspiring the next generation for Liverpool. They are the perfect role models and their impact on the club has been gigantic. I don't like them, I proper love them. The mentality monsters will attack next season again, not defend what we have.'

Lijnders believes one of the most fundamental actions for success has been keeping the group together. Under Klopp, the only player to leave Anfield that Liverpool wanted to keep was Coutinho, who had already spent five years on Merseyside. He was still sold on the club's terms and fetched the third highest fee ever at the time which was used to fortify the squad.

Bar Alisson and Van Dijk, the 'essentials' of the squad have recommitted to Liverpool and are tied down to long-term deals. The priority is to get the pedigreed goalkeeper and centre-back pairing to follow suit. Wijnaldum is in the final year of his contract and could seek a new challenge, which would be understandable at his age.

Liverpool have been able to hang on to their world-class talents, which hasn't been the case since the 90s. And, unlike before, the Coutinho episode proved that should a key player go, the recruitment team will ensure major money is banked and the roster is improved.

Klopp, though, asks, 'Why would you want to leave here? We have a sensational team with a sensational relationship and working environment. Who doesn't want this?'

9

'500 Different Ways' To Win

'I think that's what separates Liverpool from a lot of other clubs. It's not, "We won something, now we're the champs and we did it." Until we retire, we're never done . . . that shows peak performance at its finest.'   *Sebastian Steudtner,*
high-wave champion surfer

In the week leading up to the 2019 Champions League final in Madrid, James Milner posed a prophetic question in the players' meeting to talk through the lessons of previous showpieces and their approach against Tottenham. 'What happens if we get an early goal?' he asked, telling the team that just as he'd already spelled out with scoring in finals, the reaction is as important as when you concede. Milner's instructions were for Liverpool to stay on the front foot and not go into a shell of protection.

There is nothing anyone can say, however, to prepare a team — especially one that had lost their previous three cup finals and were intensely desperate to change that — for winning a penalty just 24 seconds into the match after Sadio Mane's pass struck the outstretched arm of Moussa Sissoko. When Mohamed Salah scored the second fastest goal in a Champions League final from the spot, Liverpool played within themselves. Their performance was atypical: they were not dominant, they did not own the ball. And yet, they were comfortable with Alisson only having to make a significant contribution in the late exchanges before Divock Origi's left-footed strike evaded Spurs goalkeeper Hugo Lloris and pinballed into the bottom-far corner to make sure the Reds lifted a sixth European Cup. Liverpool were the first side to win club football's greatest prize on the continent having less possession (35.4 per cent) than the opposition since Jose Mourinho's Inter Milan beat Bayern Munich in 2010. That night at the Wanda Metropolitano drilled a considerable message into the squad that had escaped them previously: you cannot always win with beauty. Sometimes you have to get over the line by being the beasts.

'I played many more finals than I won, we always played better football,' Jürgen Klopp said in his post-match analysis. 'You saw it was a fight. A final is about the result and we need to make this experience a little bit longer or more often than others. The boys showed it, the resilience and everything you need to block the decisive balls and we scored goals in the right moment.'

Liverpool had performed streets better against Real Madrid in Kiev and were losers. Now, a new mantra was born at Melwood: 'Just f***ing win.' It is myopic to assess the stellar accomplishments of this team only in the prism of the past two seasons. 'Madrid drilled home the lesson that you win by whatever means necessary whether it's pretty or not,' Adam Lallana says. 'But the process of getting to that point, of growing together in our understanding of game management, started long before that.'

It is only natural and obvious to associate Liverpool's much-improved defensive state of affairs and elevation in being streetwise to the recruitment of Virgil van Dijk in January 2018 and Alisson six months later. They have, after all, significantly transformed the club and established themselves as the best in the world in their positions.

But development is a collective process, and Klopp will preach this externally for as long as it takes for the information to sink in: that even the greatest players in the world need the right platform, conditions and teammates to succeed.

On 21 November 2017, the Reds turned out at the Ramón Sánchez Pizjuán Stadium for a Champions

League group test against Sevilla, their vanquishers in the Europa League final a year earlier. Half an hour into the encounter, an electric Liverpool were 3–0 up thanks to a Roberto Firmino brace either side of a Sadio Mane goal. Instead of controlling proceedings after having taken such a commanding lead, they continued to function on adrenaline and emotion. After the break, Wissam Ben Yedder struck twice in the space of nine minutes before Guido Pizarro dramatically secured a point for Sevilla in added-on time.

It was a failure in game management of epic proportions and the squad were absolutely livid with themselves. The senior players' committee scheduled a team meeting to have an open, honest and critical discussion focusing on why they were ignoring the manager's protection-first command and why adrenaline so often overtook their intelligence.

There was no finger-pointing, it was a collective issue and needed collective sorting. The players felt they were letting Klopp and the coaching staff down by being swayed by the shape of a match rather than using their tactical instructions to mould it themselves. These dialogues became the norm, with the 4–3 win over Manchester City at Anfield in January 2018 providing another such chance for self-reflection.

The squad felt Klopp's work on the defensive side of the game was being undermined by their inability to be more streetwise. There is an erroneous perception of the manager as a purely attack-minded, offensively chaotic master. While he enjoys his teams being entertaining, expressive and channelling their explosiveness, Klopp is actually more obsessed with protection and is rather conservative within the framework of his principles.

When he joined Liverpool, the first requirements he spelled out to the team concerned the defensive methodology. Every pre-match analytical meeting from then has started with that element: these are the opposition's strengths, here is how we guard against that while countering with our own trademarks against their weaknesses. There are tactical tweaks for every fixture, which essentially centre around Liverpool's defensive duty first and foremost.

At the end of every season, the analysts and assistant manager Peter Krawietz cut a five-minute philosophy video on the way the team is expected to play to re-enforce the tenets to the squad, but also to introduce it to new signings. The clip always begins with defensive points: high-press, counter-press, how Liverpool press into a midfield block. Only then does it go into the offensive habits. Klopp has repeatedly underscored that if the defensive side is sorted, the rest of the play flourishes from it.

Krawietz operates under the radar somewhat, never

receiving as much credit as his work deserves outside the walls of Melwood. Not that he minds, as long as his observations are acted upon. He is core to all match preparation, intervention and assessment — actions pre-match, at half-time and post-match all have his fingerprints on them.

Krawietz, supported by first-team analysts Mark Leyland, Harrison Kingston and Greg Mathieson, has been instrumental to Liverpool's powers from set-pieces both offensively and defensively. He supplies the team with all the problems they could face, the solutions and every edge they can maximise. Training sessions are then prepared around this information by Pep Lijnders.

Normally on the day before a match, Liverpool do an intense tactical session where the starting XI face off against an XI, the Yellows, that are prepped to play with key traits of the opposition: their shape, how they build up play, how they act out of possession. This allows the team to familiarise themselves with it before the game, but also leads to hugely intense battles. Klopp has often joked that the Yellows could have won the league too given their application in training. He completely believes that Liverpool would not be champions if it wasn't for the standards set by everyone in training — those on the fringes, the young players — and the insistence of showing the same zeal that they would on a matchday.

'You never, ever do a session on autopilot, whether it's a passing drill or a shooting drill — everything is reacting to the next situation,' James Milner explained to the club's website. 'If we do a shooting drill there's three or four balls going on at the same time; 'keepers are having nightmares going for one shot then straight for the next one. You're clipping a ball to someone else and as you're doing that another ball is on its way to you to shoot. The training is completely different to anything I've seen. The whole thing around it is reacting to the next situation and staying in the game. The gaffer is very good at always thinking about what might affect a game. He's very aware of what's going on around it and always tries to nip anything in the bud that might affect the team's performance or mentality going into the game. That's one of the strengths he definitely has in terms of preparing that side. Obviously, he's a great coach in how he prepares us for every game as well, but in terms of that side he's always very aware of what could stop you putting in your best performance and going into the game fully fresh mentally.'

Repetition on the training field, developing together and adding greater quality to the group are seen as the three major facets behind Liverpool being able to win in '500 different ways', as the manager put it. A team that was once framed by their attacking blurs that could obliterate opponents could now beat them without needing a blitz.

The statistics for the 2019–20 league-winning season make for interesting analysis. Liverpool showed their evolution, with 15 league victories by a one-goal margin; 19 points were recovered from trailing positions, second only to Wolves (21); there were 51 goals from open play in the top flight, five from the spot, 10 on the counter and 17 from set-pieces – the latter two being the most in the division. No team scored more headers (18) and a club record 17 different players found the back of the net in the campaign.

Liverpool's variety and tenacity saw them break the all-time best start record after 21 games in any of Europe's top five leagues, collecting a new benchmark 61 points. They equalled the feat of 32 wins in a single season, set by City in 2017–18 and 2018–19. And for the first time in the club's history, Liverpool beat every other team in the division in a single campaign.

'I think that a lot of that comes from experience and setbacks,' says captain Jordan Henderson on their evolution. 'I think it built up that mentality to keep going — not just when we've had knocks, but after big wins too. In the successful times, it's just as important that your mind is not dwelling on it and you're ready to work again. I was really confident at the start of the season because once we'd won the Champions League, it was so obvious to see and feel that this squad wanted more. The lads were really ready to put the biggest effort in again physically and mentally. Breaking through obstacles and finding a way to win has been a big strength of ours for the past two years, no matter what stage the game is at. More often than not we find a way, and different ways as well. And that's really important, you know, because football matches can change so much. You have so many things that can influence a game like the referee's decisions, VAR, injuries . . . But if you're mentally able to deal with whatever comes, you will find solutions.

'We've done that really well over the past couple of seasons. And I think that's a lot to do with experience within the game. And obviously what the manager wants us to do on the training pitch. When you're together for a long period of time, which a lot of the squad has been, that helps us understand each other and what we're all about. It's also about the manager's mentality of never giving up which he has instilled in this team.'

Evolution was paramount because competitors increasingly started to sit deep against Liverpool, nullifying their offensive weaponry. Every detail was paid attention to and maximised. The coaching staff shortened the distance between the midfield three and implemented slight tweaks to the organisation, in possession and out of it, to aid counter-pressing as well as the domination of play in the opposition half. Liverpool became more purposeful with the ball and changed the tempo of their passing.

'We develop together,' Klopp said in December 2019. 'I am not so silly that I say I only want to see a game where I only see that "blitz" football and all the rest I do not want to see. The reason we did that focus on attacking was to implement some very important things like how to press, counter-attack and use situations when we win the ball, which we still do. But of course now, especially in the last one-and-a-half years, a lot of teams sit back so we have to play around that wall. There are different ways to score a goal. There are different ways to control a game. There are different ways to finish a game off. A couple of them we showed already. A couple more we will show.'

Bar the tactical and technical alterations, a focus was also placed on widening the minds of the players. To that end, Klopp invited world-renowned high-wave surfer Sebastian Steudtner to join the club on their Evian training camp in preparation for their watershed 2019–20 season. He wanted a fresh voice, beyond the football bubble, to illustrate an 'anything is possible' outlook in a unique way. Klopp had learned about the two-time XXL Biggest Wave Award winner through a

TV documentary and was wowed by Steudtner's ability to concentrate on his task despite the pressure, expectation and circumstances.

On 1 August 2019, the fourth day at their pre-season base in the five-star Hotel Royal, with its panoramic views over Lake Geneva, the squad were gathered around the pool. Klopp introduced them to Steudtner, who shared a summary of his life story before explaining the art of training your mind to stay still regardless of the challenge.

The German, hailing from Nuremberg, asked the players to hold their breath underwater for as long as possible and the first attempts spanned between 10 to 90 seconds fully submerged. Half-an-hour later, Dejan Lovren and Mohamed Salah were underwater for nearly four minutes, with the Croatian just edging his best friend.

'If you're focused on, "I want to breathe, I want to get my head out of the water, I'm uncomfortable", you're going to panic right away and not be able to perform at all,' Steudtner explained to Liverpool's website.

'But if you relax and focus on, "Okay, I'm here, it's good, I'm doing well and I can do this", then you add that competitive edge, "Okay, I know my time and I know that the body next to me did longer than me, I need to calm down even more and focus on being relaxed." I think you can translate it to anything. They understood it really, really quick.'

Steudtner was conversely inspired by Liverpool. The European champions were not content with their success in Madrid and searched outside the box for edges.

'I think that's what separates Liverpool from a lot of other clubs — the competitive drive and the not being satisfied and always looking ahead is what drives them,' he said. 'It's not, "We won something, now we're the champs and we did it." Until we retire, we're never done. It's a challenge but it doesn't look like a challenge anymore — that shows peak performance at its finest.'

There were countless matches that encapsulated Liverpool's technical and tactical variety as well as their mental fortitude — or as Jose Mourinho termed it 'their complete puzzle' — in their title-winning campaign. The most significant came against City, in a 3–1 victory at Anfield in November, after which Henderson said, 'There's no hiding from the fact it did feel big. When you go head-to-head with your title rival and win, it does feel like a double hit.'

Liverpool bossed the midfield battle against City, with the skipper, Gini Wijnaldum and Fabinho a hybrid of destroyers and creators: physical, disciplined, press-resistant, with the latter setting the tempo of that Sunday evening with one of the goals of the season.

Liverpool's full-backs were imperious too. Trent Alexander-Arnold's diagonal pass with his weaker foot to Andy Robertson was conjured with the precision and craft of a pedigreed midfielder. The left-back took the ball, supplying a teasing cross to the far post for Mohamed Salah to head in Liverpool's second.

'I don't think I ever saw a goal like this. Probably not,' Klopp said in his analysis. 'A right full-back with a 60-yard pass to the left full-back; two more touches and a cross over 40 yards and a header. That's pretty special. It was a good moment to score a goal like this.'

Liverpool's defence was steely, only switching off to leave Bernardo Silva unmarked to pull one back for City, but that 78th-minute effort was the first shot on target they were afforded in the second half. The front three of Salah, Firmino and Mane defended excellently, contributing six tackles, eight possession gains and one clearance between them, with the Senegal international getting the third goal shortly after the break.

'They are incredibly strong in the set-pieces,' Guardiola said when he was asked why Liverpool are so hard to play against. 'When you sit back and defend in the box, they open you up with Alexander-Arnold and Robertson and start to make crosses.

'When they arrive with not just Mane, Salah, Firmino, but Henderson coming with the right tempo, Wijnaldum and the second balls, it's almost impossible to live with that situation. When you are able to get back from that position, they have an incredible back four. And when you are attacking, like we tried, every mistake you can do — the transitions are the biggest quality of Jürgen from all of his career — like the situation with the second goal.'

Liverpool were also cunning. They frustrated City by slowing the game down to prevent them taking quick throw-ins or free-kicks. They also reacted to big moments better, which stands as one of the greatest differentiating factors between the teams. When the ball struck Alexander-Arnold's arm five minutes into the game, Sergio Aguero stopped playing to appeal to referee Michael Oliver for a penalty. He was joined by Kevin De Bruyne and Silva, but the ball was still there to be won, with Raheem Sterling free on the far side and screaming for a delivery. Instead, Liverpool shifted it quickly to Mane and within 22 seconds, Fabinho had rocketed in a 'goalazo' to give them the lead.

Liverpool managed the encounter better and ulti-mately the season, too. The Merseysiders' previous league duel was at Aston Villa, where their resolve to get three points shone through again. Trezeguet supplied the hosts with a shock lead in the first half, his goal being ruled just onside, while Firmino's armpit was deemed to be offside when he had the ball in the back of the net. As the clock ticked down, it started to feel like it might need to be filed under 'just one of those days' for Liverpool.

'We made it difficult for ourselves,' Klopp said. 'We started playing football good but not exactly like we should have done. Aston Villa were ready today for a proper fight, a proper battle, defend with all they have, try to find spaces for counter-attacks and be there and have good set-pieces.

'We played good football, but didn't finish the situations and then we conceded a goal, then it is not so easy to change these wrong decisions, this wrong path, immediately. We needed a bit of time.'

Liverpool left it incredibly late, but they did alter the outcome of the match. On 87 minutes, a goal was carved out of pure determination by Mane and Robertson, with the latter heading in and running into the net to retrieve the ball so Liverpool could chase a winner.

'The right winger cuts back, crosses with his left foot and your left-back is in the six-yard box at that time of the game to score,' Klopp said. 'That's the risk you have to take. We want to play like this, it must be possible.'

With seconds remaining, Alexander-Arnold swung in a corner with Mane showing all the courage in a run to dissect Conor Hourihane and Jonathan Kodjia, taking a boot to the face in the process before guiding the ball with his head into the far corner to make it 2–1. He was assisted by Firmino obstructing several markers in a goal Klopp loved. 'Bobby blocks three players, he blocks the whole world pretty much,' he said. 'Sadio goes with his head even though there's a Villa boot in his face. It was the pure desire to score.'

Prior to both those games, Liverpool had travelled to Turf Moor and comfortably swatted Burnley aside 3–0. Klopp believed the performance represented how much the team had developed from his first experience at the ground. In August of 2016, first-half goals from Sam Vokes and Andre Gray ensured the hosts were the victors with Liverpool unable to recover after horrid defending.

That day they had 81 per cent of possession and 26 shots, but played out of desperation rather than a deep belief in their way. 'Our decision making was not good,' Klopp said at the time. 'We'd put in a good cross but there were no bodies in the box and then when we had bodies in the box we ended up shooting. We need to have a plan for deep defending teams. We have a few things to do – that is clear.'

Fast forward and Liverpool's 3–0 victory at Turf Moor captured the growth at play since Klopp's appointment. The opening 30 minutes followed the usual script of having to grind hard against well-organised, direct and uncomfortable opponents. A four-minute blitz then brought two goals, with Chris Wood deflecting in Alexander-Arnold's cross, then sublime work from Firmino leading to a fantastic Mane finish.

'Now we believe in ourselves,' Klopp said. 'We developed so much. We didn't lose patience, we stayed straightforward, we were excellent in the counter-press. You can see it's more habit now.'

The automation comes from repetition on the training pitches, overseen by Pep Lijnders, which brought greater consistency. It is also the result of the players becoming more familiar with each other as well as with the manager's demands in specific moments. Liverpool were able to explore Klopp's ideology properly in every single scenario on a football pitch over time. When Firmino makes a movement towards the ball, for example, that's a signal for two players to run behind like Salah, Mane or one of the attackers and a No 8.

'We improved so much as a team,' Lijnders says. 'We press better together, the timings and the triggers. We are much more together. Our positional game improved so much, with and without the ball. This had an enormous impact on our regularity. There is a mentality installed in the group that they see each coming game as a final. It goes so deep and stems from Jürgen's personality, the competitive training process and the stability in our squad. That's the only way: going session by session and keeping a core group together for a long period of time.

'We evolved, and that's the main reason we won the Champions League, the Super Cup, Club World Cup and now the Premier League. We can never forget where we are, how we became, it's because of the ambition, quality and attitude of our players. We want to be the team nobody wants to play against. The team who doesn't need to feel we are the best team in world football, but the team who can beat everyone. The secret is to keep the mentality.'

The manager wholly agrees. 'I saw Pep Guardiola said we won the league because we played each game like it was the last game of our lives,' Klopp notes. 'And actually, that was the plan and the boys did it. It was a bit of a shame that because of this attitude that we showed and this mentality of "next game, next game" we didn't celebrate properly all the single victories and the details that got us over the line.

'We had a very little celebration when we won the Club World Cup in Qatar. But all the other times during the season, winning 1–0, 3–1 or whatever, you come in the dressing room and it's everyone screaming "yes" and then immediately thinking and talking about the next game — "Oh, in three days we play them, we have to go again." People think we won 32 league games this season and it must have been a been a real dressing room party after each one, but it wasn't because we were really in the zone. We were in the moment, we still enjoyed it but we never got carried away.'

It is not just the players that have evolved; the decisions of the coaching staff have too. When Klopp joined Liverpool during the October international break in 2015, Brendan Rodgers had already granted the squad four days off before his sacking. The German and his former assistant Zeljko Buvac were perplexed and annoyed by the team being given so much free time when there was a short preparation window. The Bosnian–Serb was never willing to compromise with free days, but as Klopp got to grips with the physical and mental demands of English football, he believed time off to be more beneficial than pushing players beyond their limits. That thinking is supported and encouraged by Lijnders, who advocated for the team doing the first day of recovery work at home to be with their families. Emotional wellbeing is as paramount as physical conditioning. Klopp has been as adaptable as his players, who didn't just find 500 different ways to win on route to the title but created their own bit of history.

Liverpool held a 25-point lead at one stage of the campaign, which was the biggest ever in the English top-flight. Their 3–2 victory over West Ham United on 24 February 2020 was their 21st consecutive league win at Anfield, surpassing City's record of 20, achieved between 2011 and 2012. Home triumphs over Bournemouth, Crystal Palace and Villa extended the benchmark to 24.

Securing the title with seven games to spare was a new record, with Manchester United (2000–01) and City in (2017–18) doing it with five games to spare.

For all the statistics, perhaps the numbers that most signpost Liverpool's development over the course of the past two seasons is how they transformed a 25-point gap to City to an 18-point cushion over them.

'We were not close enough three years ago, a year ago we were really close,' Klopp said. 'What the boys have done in the last two-and-a-half years, the consistency they show is absolutely incredible and second to none.'

Henderson simplified such an exacting attitude by stating 'we just want to win football games', but there could never be an overestimation of what this Liverpool squad have achieved.

'I couldn't be prouder of this team and how they've reacted to so many different obstacles not only this season, but over the past few years,' the captain said.

'It's been a special journey so far, but I hope it can last a lot longer and there's a lot more to come because we can still do better and still be better.'

10

An Unprecedented Season

'It feels fitting for the 96 at Hillsborough that we're
lifting this trophy on 96 points . . . This is for you.'

Andy Robertson

Jürgen Klopp clenched both his fists, stretching his arms
high in triumph before embracing Pep Lijnders. And
then, he was lost. It was late into Thursday night, and
230 miles away, the final whistle had sounded at
Stamford Bridge leading to an 'explosion of emotion'
at the four-star Formby Hall golf resort and spa where
the Liverpool contingent had gathered. Chelsea had
beaten Manchester City 2–1 and Liverpool, 23 points
clear at the summit, were confirmed as league title
winners for the first time in 30 years.

As the clock struck 22.10, their status as champions
of England confirmed, Klopp temporarily lost control of

his senses. 'The moment we became champions, I had never felt a bigger relief in my life, because it was like everything — all the effort, all the planning, all the knocks — just everything came together to give the club the trophy it most wanted and waited so long for,' he says.

'I didn't expect that, to be honest. I didn't know how I would feel, but I didn't imagine it would be like that.' Seconds before the final whistle went in west London, Klopp had called his wife and sons, leaving his phone on the table with its speaker activated so they could listen in to the celebrations and feel part of it. But he couldn't recount what he did in the seconds after referee Stuart Attwell signalled the end of the game until watching LFCTV's *Golden Sky* documentary a few days later.

'Ricky [Mears, the club's lead cameraman] was there with us recording the whole day, he got all the reactions, thank goodness, so I could see what happened,' Klopp laughs. 'I saw the footage in one of the documentaries where I'm standing next to Pep [Lijnders], we hug each other and then I'm just walking through completely lost. I really don't know what was happening. I couldn't connect in that moment, I was in another world. Everybody was hugging and screaming and celebrating and I was just there thinking where to go with all these feelings and emotions now. Wow. It was incredibly, incredibly special.

'Then I tried to call Ulla and she didn't pick up the phone because in that moment they got a big parcel from Liverpool that all the families received. So then I phoned my son because they were all together. I wanted to talk, but I couldn't. I was just crying. It was unbelievable. I cannot describe it. What I realised then was how deep the relief was. It is the one thing everybody wanted us to win. And because everybody wants you to win something, that doesn't mean it will happen. So, so, so many things had to come together that we actually had the chance to win it. And then we did it. That's a pretty big one. And that was absolutely, absolutely special.'

On the night before these intoxicating scenes on 25 June 2020, Liverpool had delivered an irresistible, assured display by demolishing Crystal Palace 4–0 at Anfield. Their focus was so concentrated on the match that they hadn't considered what they would do if victory was secured, giving them the chance to win the league without having to kick a ball when Chelsea hosted City.

The directive for the defending champions was to not drop points at Stamford Bridge, but while they were favourites for the encounter, there was still a great possibility that the offensive aggression of Frank Lampard's men could hurt them. And so on the morning of the blockbuster clash, Klopp decided that all the staff and players regularly tested for coronavirus had to be together. Attendance was compulsory because the manager reasoned 'whoever stays at home and watches it alone will regret it for the rest of their life'.

An expansive barbecue was prepared at Formby Hall, with everyone sitting out on the terrace enjoying the food and a relaxed atmosphere as Arsenal eased past Southampton at St Mary's in the earlier fixture. The intensity was immediately heightened once City lined up against Chelsea, with all eyes seared to the gigantic screen set up outside. 'The concentration was like we were playing,' Klopp laughs.

City had edged the opening half hour, but then gifted their hosts an advantage after a horrid defensive lapse. Benjamin Mendy and Ilkay Gündogan were slack, leaving the ball for each other only for Christian Pulisic to glide in and take it under his spell near the halfway line.

Liverpool's players were off their seats, on their feet and urging him on. The USA international motored forward, skinning Mendy and sending a curved finish around goalkeeper Ederson. The Reds celebrated that 36th-minute strike as though it was a goal the team had scored themselves, but it was still so early and the opposition were City after all.

As expected, Guardiola's side shot back. A needless foul by N'Golo Kanté offered Kevin De Bruyne the opportunity to apply his sorcery to a set-piece and he duly obliged. He directed a dipping free-kick into the top corner from 25-yards to level the contest and quieten the cheers at Formby Hall.

The game gave rise to plenty of nerves on the hotel's terrace, but it was a certified thriller and the prime spectacle of the behind-closed-doors contests after the coronavirus-enforced shutdown of football. So, naturally, twists were expected. Raheem Sterling could only chip against the post at the end of a stunning counter-attack, and Kyle Walker scrambled the ball off the line after Pulisic had rounded Ederson in the City goal.

That clearance prompted Liverpool goalkeeper Alisson to get up and declare he couldn't handle watching anymore, but before he could make it inside, Chelsea had launched another foray forward.

In a hectic scramble inside the City six-yard area, Ederson thwarted Tammy Abraham, Fernandinho blocked Pulisic's follow-up, but then used his hand to deny Abraham again. The commentary at Formby Hall was simple yet emphatic. 'PENALTY!' the players cried before greeting the replay with a communal 'RED CARD!' Both of their calls were confirmed by the video assistant referee; Fernandinho was sent off and Willian stepped up to convert a fine spot-kick on 78 minutes.

The clock was ticking but time appeared to stand

still on Merseyside, the desperation to hear the final whistle hanging heavy in the air. Finally, injury-time was almost up and Liverpool's players and staff started doing a countdown unlike any other: a 30-year wait was to be over in 10 seconds. And then, relief combined with rapture to create a memory none of them will ever forget. The title was not won at Anfield, or on any pitch. It was not won in front of fans. It was not won the way anyone would have imagined it. But it was won — after a season where Liverpool's resilience and unyielding nature put them in a different league to everyone else, with a global pandemic threatening to render that meaningless when they needed just two points to be champions. Their determination to 'just win, win, win' was unbelievable and the circumstances were unprecedented.

'Campione, campione, ole ole ole,' Liverpool's players and staff belted out before the scale of the achievement started to take hold. Captain Jordan Henderson put his sunglasses on to partially disguise his tear-soaked face, while full-backs Trent Alexander-Arnold and Andy Robertson hugged each other for an extended period, the former then using his champions scarf to wipe his eyes. It was fitting that Formby Hall was the scene for all of them — the same venue Klopp had made it compulsory to attend the 2015 Christmas party after losing to Watford. They had travelled so far, so furiously.

Despite it being almost certain since January that Liverpool would be England's kings, no one knew how to process what had just happened. Adam Lallana deconstructs a Thursday like no other. 'It started off as a normal day and I remember thinking, "Ah, we've got this barbecue later to watch the match." Not one time did it come into my head that we could potentially win the league that evening,' he says. 'It just didn't come into my head, whether I just thought that City would win or not allowing myself to get so far ahead, I don't know. But my feeling was, "Yes, a barbecue with the lads to watch the match. That's going to be really nice." So when it actually happened, there were all these hard-to-explain emotions that I don't think any of us expected. You saw the boss getting upset, Jordan was really emotional. I remember going to the toilet and my hands were just shaking a little bit. And that must've just been all the built up relief, joy, happiness, gratitude all in one.

'The day was probably as perfect as it could have been. If it happened at a game we were playing, not everyone would have been able to be there in terms of staff and players because of the restriction on numbers. But at Formby Hall we were all together, each person who played a part — whether it was the young lads keeping the energy up in training or the physios who made sure we were ready — to share in the special achievement. We enjoyed each other's company, we had drinks and just tried to make the most out of celebrating in challenging times. As I'm sitting in my car now, I still cannot believe the season we've had. Thinking through it blows my mind.'

Liverpool reported for 2019–20 as champions of Europe and the theme all throughout pre-season was to extend that remit to England. 'Producing the Champions League made us winners and we got the feeling for it,' Andy Robertson said the afternoon after the milestone night before. With heavy eyes, a sore head and hoarse voice from the Formby Hall festivities he admitted the players weren't shy to insist nothing less than winning the title would do.

'We came back in pre-season as if this year is going to be our year for the Premier League, we are going to make it our year, and we are going to go out and do it,' Robertson added. 'We are going to show everyone we can win the league, and we can go again and get the better of Man City this time and not be behind them. We showed that from the get-go, from day one.'

Trying to oust Guardiola's machine, a City team that completely reconfigured what it takes to win the league by amassing a combined 198 points over the previous two seasons, required Liverpool to be 'near perfect' in

Klopp's estimation. Such a push could only be under-pinned by the right attitude, total commitment and a rare sort of relentlessness. 'The players didn't come to pre-season singing that they were champions of Europe,' John Achterberg says. 'The mentality from the first session was, "Okay, we have to be better, we have to be more consistent, we have to give absolutely everything again and more if we want to win the league."'

Liverpool had a big meeting during pre-season where the squad and the coaching staff discussed the aims for the campaign and made a pact that they would do whatever it takes to become champions of England. 'Every training session felt like it was the most impor-tant of our lives,' Klopp says. 'That is the desire and the determination the boys showed. They were switched on from the second they all came back to Melwood after the holidays and knew we were amazing points-wise in 2018–19, but we still had space to improve performance-wise and they all wanted to do that.'

The first opportunity to show the outside world a snapshot of this was on 9 August 2020, with promoted Norwich City the visitors to Anfield. Daniel Falke's men were too expansive and were ruthlessly punished for it with Liverpool 3–0 up inside half an hour cour-tesy of a Grant Hanley own goal and efforts from Mohamed Salah and Virgil van Dijk.

Liverpool were purring and enjoying a statement start

to the season before being hit with an almighty sucker punch. Alisson was shaping up to take a quick free-kick, slipped and lay in agony clutching his right calf. The world's best goalkeeper had to be replaced on 38 minutes and coming on for him was Adrian, who had been training at semi-professional side Unión Deportiva Pilas in Spain's sixth tier with personal goalkeeping coach Pedro Illanes and a physical trainer just a few weeks earlier.

The Spaniard, whose contract at West Ham United had expired, was on the verge of accepting an offer from Real Valladolid before receiving a 'bombshell' call from Liverpool, who had sold Simon Mignolet and required a back-up in goal.

Adrian joined the club four days before the Norwich game and hadn't even undertaken a handful of training sessions when he was called into action. Alisson's injury prompted some in the media to suggest Liverpool's tilt at the title could have been significantly damaged before it even properly started, but that wasn't to be the case.

The Brazilian international would be sidelined for 67 days and the victories rolled on. Throughout the campaign, there had been a narrative playing out suggesting that Liverpool were lucky not to have had any of their key players sidelined for lengthy periods, which was actually in opposition to reality. Fabinho, the defensive midfield maestro, was unavailable for 53 days with an ankle injury, captain Henderson missed only 10 fewer with a hamstring problem and Joel Matip was absent for over three months.

Having just come into the team, Adrian was in danger of being on the treatment table too. Liverpool's second task of the season was a trip to Turkey to contest the Super Cup against Chelsea at Beşiktaş Park. In that showdown, the veteran filtered the highs and lows of a goalkeeper into a manic 120 minutes. Adrian produced a crucial save at the feet of Mateo Kovacic, before being beaten by Giroud's low finish, which skidded underneath him. He did superbly to deny Tammy Abraham with his feet in extra-time, but was adjudged to have impeded the 20-year-old in the area before being sat down by Jorginho's ice-cool technique from the resulting penalty, which forced a shootout.

Adrian denied Mason Mount late on and decisively saved Abraham's spot-kick to crown Liverpool as Super Cup winners. And as if more couldn't have happened to him in such a short space of time, the 32-year-old hurt his ankle when a supporter breached the barricade during the post-match celebrations and ran across the pitch to evade security guards before slipping and clattering into him.

On the four-and-a-half-hour flight back to Liverpool, head physio Lee Nobes worked on the swollen area to ensure Adrian would pass a late fitness test to start at Southampton. At St Mary's, Sadio Mane and Roberto Firmino gave the Reds a 2–0 cushion, but on 83 minutes, the keeper's clearance from Van Dijk's back pass ricocheted off Danny Ings' shin and into the net. It led to a tense finish on the south coast, but Liverpool held out.

'No problem with that as long as we win the games,' was Klopp's reaction and victories became habitual for Liverpool. By the time they set off to Qatar on 15 December for the Club World Cup, which many observers believed would halt their runaway form in the league given a packed schedule (12 games in five different competitions over six weeks), they were 10 points clear of second-placed Leicester City.

No team had beaten them in the top flight and Manchester United were the only side to manage a draw against the Reds. Arsenal, Leicester, Tottenham, Everton and City left Anfield with nothing while Chelsea were bettered at Stamford Bridge.

But the complication of dealing with the Club World Cup was furthered by a young Liverpool side beating the Gunners 5–4 on penalties in the League Cup fourth round after a riotously entertaining 5–5 draw. The quarter-final of the competition was scheduled the night before the club were due to kick off their exploits in Qatar.

Playing two matches in two continents within 24 hours was a tricky situation to solve. Liverpool Under-23 coach Neil Critchley, now manager of Blackpool, took charge of an academy team — the average age of the starting XI was 19.5 years — at Aston Villa with the entire senior squad away. The young Reds gave a good account of themselves in possession, but were given a 5–0 lesson in having a clinical edge by their seasoned opponents.

In February, Critchley would again be in the dugout guiding a youthful outfit in an FA Cup replay at Shrewsbury Town. This time, Liverpool were 1–0 victors but Klopp's decision-making around these cup matches was widely slated.

'Look, at the start of the season we ignored the fact we had so many games with the Club World Cup and having to travel there, we knew we just had to find a way to deal with it,' Klopp says. 'But then, in the season — another game, another game. The boys cannot play two games in 24 hours in two different continents, it is not possible and not smart. We didn't become famous for our decisions, for choosing to use the kids and stuff like that. We had no chance to do it any other way with Villa and Shrewsbury because of the number of games we had. We had to focus in a specific moment on specific competitions and we couldn't just play the games because they were there. During this period, when there were more matches than training, what Mona [Nemmer, head of nutrition] and Korny [Andreas Kornmayer, head of fitness and conditioning] did was just incredible and helped us massively with recovery between the games.

'You don't really train in those moments. We had longer meetings than training sessions. Before we went to Qatar, I couldn't expect or imagine how cool it is to play the Club World Cup. Next to our hotel was another one with a rooftop bar and Flamengo's supporters were there celebrating for three or four days constantly. It was a bit annoying from a noise point of view, but it showed me just how big the tournament is to the rest of the world. When I asked my Brazilian players about it, they were so desperate to win it. Lots of people thought we would be out of gas when we came from Qatar, too tired to carry on. But actually, it gave us energy. Now we were champions of the world and the players really enjoyed that.'

A 2–1 win over Mexico's Monterrey was followed by Firmino scoring the only goal in the final against Flamengo giving Liverpool their first-ever Club World Cup triumph — a piece of silverware that eluded them in 1981, 1984 (then the Intercontinental Cup) and 2005. 'World and European Champions. That's got a nice ring to it,' James Milner tweeted in the immediate aftermath. The most coveted label was still to come.

Liverpool returned from Qatar and had four days to prepare for the Boxing Day blockbuster with Leicester, who were positioned as their closest title rivals. The battle at the King Power Stadium was being billed as the match that could spark a slip from Klopp's men given their exertions.

Harrison Kingston, the club's head of post-match analysis, created a short video on the plane journey back from Qatar featuring the elements of play that made the team what they are, demonstrating the squad's quality, character and power. It was a clever way to re-energise the group. Liverpool bounced into town and bulldozed former manager Brendan Rodgers' side in mesmerising fashion.

A Firmino double, a penalty from Milner and a sweet right-foot angled finish from Trent Alexander-Arnold pulverised Leicester, who were not in the same stratosphere as their visitors in or out of possession. It was the biggest margin of victory in a clash between teams starting the day in the top two of the Premier League since leaders City beat United 6–1 in October 2011. 'People were trying to put us in a race with Liverpool, but we know where we are,' Rodgers said.

The Merseysiders edged Wolves 1–0 at Anfield in their final test of 2019, ending the year having earned 98 points from 37 league matches. Their ratio of 2.65 points per game was the second highest achieved by a team in a calendar year in the competition after Chelsea's 2.66 in 2005.

On 19 January 2020, after not losing a match in England's top flight for 381 days, the Kop finally allowed themselves to let go, loudly declaring, *'And now you're gonna believe us. We're gonna win the league.'* It took reaching 64 points, going 16 clear at the top with a game in hand, and a goal at the death from Salah against Manchester United, the old enemy, for that chorus to be heard from Liverpool fans for the first time in the season.

Henderson was on the pitch handling post-match media duties as the chant reached its crescendo. 'We're not really thinking about the end,' he said. 'Why should we change now? For us, as players, it's the next game, the next challenge and the Premier League's tough.'

For the fans, though, it felt right to indulge themselves. They were witnessing greatness, having seen their side lose just once in 623 days. That statistic never looked under threat against United at Anfield.

'They can sing whatever they want — apart from my name before the game is finished! I'm not here to dictate what they have to sing,' Klopp said. 'If our fans would not be in a good mood now, that would be really strange. The only thing that I can tell you is that we are here to work.

'The fans are allowed to dream, to sing — as long

as they do their job as well in the moment when we play, all fine. We will not be part of that party yet, but it is not a problem because we know our job.'

Van Dijk added, 'I think everyone wants us to say something about the title, but we won't. We won't get carried away. We cannot, and we won't.'

Throughout the campaign, Liverpool had showcased a strength in doing whatever was necessary to win: there were the recoveries which included the late equaliser at Old Trafford, victory against Tottenham at Anfield, the win at Villa Park. Resilience was in deep supply too: keeping out Jose Mourinho's charges in North London, the grit at Sheffield United, the almighty battle at Molineux, seeing off Norwich away, the rally to overcome West Ham 3–2.

Their ceaseless attitude was not just appreciated in England. Julian Nagelsmann, the most coveted manager in Europe and at the helm of RB Leipzig, told the *Independent*: 'If you want to be a good manager, you have to watch Liverpool games. What they are doing is incredible. It's the performances that you can learn from, but more importantly, is what you can take away from their mentality. It's totally crazy when you're so successful, you're so many points ahead of the next team in the league, but you do more and more and more to win games. That is a big message to give to players, especially the young ones.

'They should learn from Liverpool to always be hungry, to be better. It doesn't matter if you're nearly the champion, you still win and win and win and win.'

In the group stages of the Champions League, Liverpool had lost 2–0 away to Napoli on 17 September and the senior side would only be beaten again in February, five months later, at Atletico Madrid in the last-16 of the same competition. They were human after all. But by the end of that month, they were served their first league defeat of the season in an embarrassing 3–0 capitulation against Watford at Vicarage Road. A second-half double from the explosive Ismaïla Sarr was complemented by a Troy Deeney effort to scar the champions-in-waiting. A rotated Liverpool exited the FA Cup at the hands of Chelsea in their next fixture, with the team again failing to get on the scoresheet and goals from Willian and Ross Barkley doing the damage.

They were vanquished again eight days later, and while the ultimate result was the same, everything was different. Atleti were the slayers in Europe again, but the circumstances around the Anfield encounter were both strange and uncomfortable. Diego Simeone's men defeated Liverpool 3–2 in that second leg to secure their progress to the Champions League quarter-finals in front of 3,000 travelling Atleti supporters.

They were allowed to make the journey over from Madrid despite matches in the top two divisions in Spain being played behind closed doors while nurseries, schools and universities were shut due to Covid-19. The country had reported 1,646 cases of the virus at the time, with 782 stemming from the capital. All public events involving more than 1,000 people were banned in Madrid given the escalation of the coronavirus spread, yet Atleti fans were welcomed in England.

Liverpool only had six confirmed coronavirus cases when the European tie, played in front of 54,000, went ahead on 11 March 2020. Figures close to the end of April showed 246 recorded deaths in Liverpool NHS hospitals from Covid-19. An official inquiry was launched by the City Council to ascertain whether there was a direct link between the staging of the game and the massive spike.

Klopp admitted he was uneasy in the build-up to the tussle with Atleti given the global situation, but more especially the lockdown in Madrid. 'I usually don't struggle with things around me, I can build barriers right and left when I prepare for a game, but in that moment it was really difficult,' he told the club's website.

The irregularity of matters would intensify. That match was the last Liverpool played for 102 days as the pandemic caused the suspension of all elite football in England. Uncertainty reigned supreme and while the toll on society was the most fundamental issue, the season was also in jeopardy. On a wider scale, countless jobs and the very existence of several clubs in the pyramid were at stake.

Richard Masters, the Premier League's chief executive, warned that the industry was 'losing revenue at an unprecedented level,' adding, 'the very heavy losses that we face will have to be dealt with or else clubs and other enterprises who depend on football for income will go out of business.'

Greg Clarke, chairman of the Football Association, added that the game faced 'economic challenges beyond the wildest imagination of those who run it. We face the danger of losing clubs and leagues as finances collapse. Many communities could lose the clubs at their heart with little chance of resurrection'.

There were an overflow of crucial reasons to complete the league season, yet some officials at the bottom end of the league, like West Ham's Karren Brady, were pushing for the campaign to be made null and void from March. Such concrete takes on the situation when so much was up in the air jarred with many. The sentiment of cancelling the season entirely was only properly killed in May as the Bundesliga became the first major league to return to action and provided a template to conduct training and fixtures safely.

From March to then, however, there was a mix of

anger, anxiety and disbelief at Liverpool over the tone and ferocity from so many quarters to kill off the season. 'When we were in lockdown and people started discussing the null and void thing — I don't get angry a lot to be honest, but I felt this kind of anger because of how can they judge the situation like that? I actually felt it physically,' Klopp says. 'The virus hit and hurt the whole world. We have to care for others and we also have to find a way forward to rebuild. Some of the things should have just not existed like the null and void talk. If it actually happened that would have been unbelievably hard to take. I am used to accepting knocks in life and football, many of them, but it would have been especially hard because the boys didn't just invest in this season, the consistency they showed for two and a half years was just incredible and deserved to be rewarded with the title.'

Ultimately, Liverpool had confidence that the season would resume when it was safe to do so given all the financial implications at play. And so they focused their energy in ensuring their nutrition, conditioning and team spirit was still at the highest possible level.

Mona Nemmer created a food delivery system from scratch for groceries, meals and recipes so the players didn't need to go out to do their shopping and could fully adhere to government regulations without being at risk. Andreas Kornmayer fitted each player's home with the required fitness equipment, regularly drafted fresh individual programmes as well as group routines, while yoga over Zoom became a staple for the squad. The physios were on call if any aches or pains were felt, solving any issue over video calls. The doctors Jim Moxon and Sarah Lindsay dealt with any fears or queries, while psychologist Lee Richardson was on hand to help with the anxiety of coping with an alien situation and the sudden absence of routine and purpose.

Beyond ensuring the squad were in prime physical and mental shape, Klopp was determined to ensure the emotional bond that everyone shared was still strong. A gigantic WhatsApp group was created with everyone from the training complex included and the players enjoyed what Lallana described as 'having Melwood and the dressing room at home'.

When training was allowed again under strict government protocol, Ray Haughan, the player liaison officer, completely reconfigured Melwood, making it a one-way system and creating outdoor tented gyms, changing and toilet facilities.

There was light at the end of all this work and all the waiting, with Liverpool resuming action on 21 June with a Merseyside derby at Goodison Park in football's new normal — bio-secure games behind closed-doors. Alisson's late brilliance secured a point against Everton as he kept out Dominic Calvert-Lewin's close-range flick, before Tom Davies' strike from the loose ball hit the post.

For all the change — terraces covered by flags rather than fans, temperature checks, sanitised balls, water breaks being turned into tactical interventions, five substitutions and such — there are some things that just stick. Seven of the last eight Merseyside derbies in the league at Goodison had ended in a draw so that goalless result wasn't too surprising.

In their first Anfield match back, with the Kop carpeted in the banners that usually sway in the crowd, Liverpool were phenomenal. Crystal Palace could only admire their total football while getting tanked 4–0 by it. Alexander-Arnold's sublime free-kick, Salah's slick finish, a Fabinho thunderbolt and Sadio Mane's clinical breakaway decorated what Klopp labelled an 'exceptional performance' that 'showed a lot, if not everything, what helped us into the position we are in now'.

He had given his players a very simple message. 'I said to the boys, "I want to see actually the best behind-closed-doors football ever." I'm not sure if it was the best football but it was, for sure, the best counter-pressing behind closed doors ever,' Klopp said post-match. 'We showed our supporters the respect they deserve, that we can play like they are here, even when they are not here. Yes, they can push us to incredible things and without them it's nothing close like it is when they are here.'

It was a display of champions, and the next night they would be crowned while team bonding at Formby Hall. The players were given two days off after the celebrations, leading into a clash with City at the Etihad. Guardiola's men had surrendered their crown without much fight and were desperate to deliver a statement on their own turf. They certainly did. Salah hit the post early on, but a penalty from Kevin De Bruyne and goals by Raheem Sterling and Phil Foden put City completely out of sight by half-time. Individual errors were costing Liverpool and the scoreline was further ballooned in the hosts' favour with Sterling making it 4–0 midway through the second period.

'It's a reminder of how good Man City is,' Klopp said. 'I didn't need that, that's true, because I knew it before. Still the surprise is, and it's nice that, in a league where City is playing it's possible that somebody else can be champion because that's not really likely with the quality they have.'

Wins against Aston Villa and Brighton were followed by a 1–1 draw with Burnley, which ended Liverpool's hopes of completing the season with a 100 per cent Premier League home record. The Reds then lost 2–1 to Arsenal at the Emirates, before the occasion they had waited a month for: the final Anfield fixture of the season and the chance to finally lift the trophy they had so painfully pined for.

Chelsea were the visitors and an exhilarating 5–3 exhibition won by Liverpool preceded the main act. The fireworks on the outskirts of the stadium began long before the celebrations. Then after the final whistle, Anfield went dark, red beams glistening across the terraces. For all the props, the most important element of the night, bar the trophy, was stationed in the Main Stand. Liverpool had pushed for the families and close friends of the players and staff to be at the ground and a late decision from the local Safety Advisory Group allowed an extra 200 people to attend the ceremony. 'It is amazing to have our families here,' Alexander-Arnold said at the time. 'They are the ones you play for, the people who have been there for you when things were bad. We want to thank the Premier League, the council, the government.'

It was the Melwood support staff, draped in banners reading 2019–20 Premier League Champions, that filtered onto the pitch first. They stood in front of The Kop, looking up at the podium that was enveloped by banners in the famed stand.

Klopp was called onto the stage, 1,749 days after he first arrived at Anfield, and declared Liverpool needed to 'turn from doubters to believers now'. They were transformed beyond belief. 'We are champions of

England, Europe and the world,' he emphasised. His coaching staff — Peter Krawietz, Pep Lijnders, John Achterberg, Jack Robinson and Vitor Matos — were next to receive their medals.

'I was never on The Kop before,' Klopp reflected. 'It was pretty special and I think it makes sense in the moment when the people are not in that we use The Kop to celebrate it with them together in our hearts. It was really good.'

The spotlight then turned to Liverpool's squad, who were all sporting Champions 2019–20 shirts, marked with a gold Premier League trophy on the back of it. The man of the moment, Henderson, had picked up a knee injury at Brighton earlier in the month. Klopp's instruction to him was to ensure the first part of his rehab focused on the midfielder being strong enough to do his trademark shuffle.

He did not disappoint and so after exchanging warm words from the legendary Kenny Dalglish, who signed him for Liverpool in 2011, it was time. Henderson picked up the trophy, gave it a small peck and then applied the full shuffle treatment.

'The build-up to it, walking up there was amazing,' he said. 'Winning the Premier League's been a dream of mine since I was a kid.'

As he sprung up, Anfield erupted, the night sky was turned red with flames framing the stage. Klopp had his hand on one end of the trophy and asked Lallana to grab the other side and lift it up with him — it was a symbolic moment. The midfielder, leaving as a free agent after six years at the club, had been so important for the manager when he first came in and helped set the standards at Melwood. It was a show of appreciation and the best kind of goodbye.

Over the tannoy, 'You'll Never Walk Alone' started and the manager led a powerful rendition with the squad and staff all linking arms. The euphoria continued to stream in, some of it tinged in poignancy. 'It feels fitting for the 96 at Hillsborough that we're lifting this trophy on 96 points,' Robertson tweeted. 'This is for you.'

It was a night no one could forget in a season no one could forget.

11

Leaving A Legacy

'What is the point if you are not creating a time you can remember for the rest of your life and giving the club benefits to feel long after you have left?'   *Jürgen Klopp*

'Decades from now, this club will still be talking about Jürgen and what he's built here.'
                                                    Adam Lallana

'Your personality runs right throughout the whole club . . . I'll forgive you for waking me up at 3.30 am to tell me you have won the league!'
                                    Sir Alex Ferguson to Klopp

Jürgen Klopp's understanding of a manager's role is simple: build the club, build the people, build a legacy.

Trophies are important, but not as critical as creating a sustainable way to keep securing them. Silverware is a great reward for effort, but what sticks are the shared experiences and unifying endeavours to spark something special, something lasting.

There is excitement when a new man is unveiled at the helm, but football is unforgiving and they are often ushered out the back door when they leave. That is why Klopp regularly repeats his belief that 'it's not so important what people think when you come in, it's much more important what people think when you leave' — words he used at Mainz, Borussia Dortmund and still holds true at Liverpool.

The first two clubs still view Klopp as their own and believe what they are now is owed to what he did there. On the afternoon of 23 May 2008, when he held a mic on stage in the centre of Mainz and failed to hold back the tears as he bid goodbye to the team he'd served for 19 years of his life, the crowd chanted *'Jürgen! Jürgen! Jürgen!'*

He had given them so much beyond football. There was the ride to survival during his first months in charge in the 2000–01 season when the club were doomed for the drop to Regionalliga, then Germany's third division. Mainz won six of Klopp's first seven games in charge to avert that travesty. Over the next two campaigns, he would mould the squad into a high-pressing, annoying-to-play-against machine. The club had limited players, but an elite work ethic. They would miss out on promotion to the Bundesliga by the most painful of margins — a point and then goal difference.

The day after the second time of going so close, Klopp told fans at a gathering in the city, 'I've been thinking about yesterday and decided that it must have happened for a good reason. And I've decided that someone, somewhere wanted to show to the world that when you get knocked down, not once, not twice but even three or four times, that you can get up again and keep fighting. And that person decided there is no better town to show this to the world than Mainz.'

They believed. The following season, they would finally crack promotion to the top tier. Mainz were transformed under Klopp's charge, in terms of status and psychologically. He gave the club an identity, imbued them with fighting spirit, enhanced their structures and opened them up to commercial opportunities. Klopp made the job attractive for Thomas Tuchel to develop in, before he also went on to manage Borussia Dortmund and later star-studded Paris Saint-Germain, and gave Mainz a sense of pride in themselves.

As his former Mainz teammate Thomas Ziemer explained, 'When we played in 1994, it was a really small club. But now it's one of the top clubs in Germany.

They have a new stadium, a lot of money, a good junior team — Andre Schurrle and Neven Subotic came from the youth club. It was all from Jürgen's hard work.'

On 1 October 2019, Mainz supporters unfurled a banner at the Opel Arena as a nod to their former manager being named the Best FIFA Men's Coach that year. It read, 'For us it was clear all the time, now it is official: Jürgen Klopp is the best in the world.'

During his seven years at his next club, Borussia Dortmund, Klopp transformed a club reeling from financial woes into an exhilarating global force — breaking Bayern Munich's monopoly on the Bundesliga and establishing them as regulars to Europe's top table.

In his book *Real Love: A Life with BVB*, the club's CEO Hans-Joachim Watzke revealed Klopp's decision to leave cut deep. 'We did not try to change his mind anymore. But that was maybe a mistake,' he wrote. 'Perhaps it would have been better if we had exchanged the entire team — not the coach.

'Because I knew that, we would never get back such a coach. When I said goodbye, real tears came. Such a relationship, as I had with Jürgen over seven years at BVB, that did not exist before. And such a relationship will probably never happen again.'

Dortmund still pine for Klopp, so much so that Watzke tried to lure him back after he led Liverpool to Champions League glory. 'I knew that Jürgen would decline,' he notes, 'but I would never have forgiven myself for not asking him at that moment.' The BVB that we know, that we are intoxicated by, that can attract the likes of Jadon Sancho and Erling Haaland, is a product of Klopp's hands.

Robert Lewandowski, the forward who would have lifted the Ballon d'Or in 2020 if the awards had been not cancelled, has worked under Pep Guardiola, Carlo Ancelotti, Jupp Heynckes and Hansi Flick, but had no hesitation in picking Klopp as his favourite manager. It was the 53-year-old who transformed him from an unknown Polish youngster into a world-class phenomenon. Lewandowski was almost 22 when he joined BVB in the summer of 2010, his first spell out of his homeland. He arrived at the Westfalenstadion from Lech Poznan unsure of himself, and departed the club having registered 102 goals and 42 assists in 186 competitive games under Klopp.

They won a domestic double in 2012, the DFL Supercup in 2013 and 2014, as well as reaching the 2012–13 Champions League final together. 'What I learned from him is the belief I could play at the highest level,' Lewandowski told Uefa. 'He had this influence and it helped me take the next step. He made me realise that I had more potential than even I had imagined. He could see something in me that I couldn't see.'

When Liverpool signed Takumi Minamino from Red Bull Salzburg in January 2019, he received a tweet from another one of Klopp's former players, Shinji Kagawa. 'Congrats! You are starting a great challenge,' the fellow Japan international typed. 'Believe in yourself and do your best under the best manager in the world!'

Supporters, chief executives, superstar players . . . no one is exempt from being bowled over by the Klopp effect. Or as Dortmund's Marco Reus better termed it, 'It's impossible to escape his spell, but then, why would you want to?'

Liverpool is Klopp's hat-trick — a third club completely indebted to him and enamoured of him. 'Decades from now, this club will still be talking about Jürgen and what he's built here,' Adam Lallana says. 'He walked into probably the hardest job in football and I can't imagine another manager making as big an impact — and not just in terms of winning, across all of the club.'

Liverpool legend Jamie Carragher's autobiography in 2009 asked, in a tone of hopelessness, who could possibly lead the club to the title. The former defender turned TV pundit would repeat the question every few years. He could not see any golden sky after the storm. Manchester City and Chelsea were supercharged by the financial might of their owners. Manchester United could absorb expensive mistakes and march on in their guise as a commercial behemoth. Leicester were a

5,000–1 miracle and the seven men that preceded Klopp at Anfield all had flaws that were picked at.

Graeme Souness was too hard. Roy Evans was too soft. Gérard Houllier was too stuck in his ways. Rafael Benitez rotated too much. Roy Hodgson was all wrong right from the start. Kenny Dalglish was out of top management for too long during his second stint. Brendan Rodgers hadn't been in top management long enough.

Just as Dalglish's resignation on 22 February 1991 is labelled the significant moment when Liverpool fell from their perch — most of their wounds self-inflicted, contrary to Sir Alex Ferguson's claim of knocking the club off it — Klopp's appointment on 8 October 2015 will be filed as the moment a dormant giant shook from slumber.

The German implemented an unmistakable identity, changed the psychology of the club, elevated the operation at Melwood, gave the staff responsibility and self-confidence, stirred a squad of mentality monsters, created a smoother pathway from the academy to the first team and put trophies on the board, chiefly returning the status of England's best to Liverpool.

'For me, he's up there with the great Bill Shankly,' Lallana says. 'The transformation around the whole place — the players, the staff, the fans — and the competition Liverpool have been up against really makes this so historic. I back the club to bag a few more trophies under him too and he's made sure some great young players are coming through. Then you think about the extension of Anfield and the new training complex . . . Jürgen's legacy will be the stuff of legend.'

During Klopp's first week in the job, he travelled to Kirkby to watch Liverpool's Under-18s take on Stoke City in the league at the academy base. On the balcony of the complex, he discussed the youth setup with director Alex Inglethorpe, Michael Beale, who was the Under-21 manager and Pep Lijnders, then the first-team development coach.

He enjoyed the talent on display, but had conversed with Peter Krawietz, also in attendance, about how counter-productive it was to have the academy and senior squad at two different locations separated by a five-mile distance. He spoke to Mike Gordon about finding ways to change that, affording Liverpool a training facility that wasn't only united but among the best on the continent.

The club were sold by his pitch and explored their options. Pretty quickly, it became obvious that Klopp cared considerably about every area of the club. 'When you sit in the main chair like I sit, you have a lot of power, but even more than that, you have all the responsibility,' he said.

'And responsibility for me means it never ends, even

when you leave. You need to create something where you can really be measured by, even after you've gone. You are so busy planning for the next game, but you also have to take the minutes to think and talk about changing the structure to make it more effective.

'Build this, improve that. I'm interested in everything, in the whole club and when I leave at some point, I don't want people to celebrate me still, I only want that they can still feel the benefit of me being manager here.'

The final touches are being put to a state-of-the-art complex in Kirkby, with Klopp's influence all over the £50 million building. When discussions were held with London-based architects KSS over the project, the manager's vision was central. Inspiration was drawn from Red Bull Salzburg's pioneering academy facility, with Klopp, Inglethorpe and Michael Edwards having regular dialogue and recon missions with their Austrian counterparts.

The influence can be seen in the crisp, modern layout of Liverpool's new base, with the floor-to-ceiling windows encouraging plenty of natural light. The large indoor sports hall, hydrotherapy area, open-plan recovery rooms and specialist sports rehabilitation suites are a nod to the facilities seen at Salzburg. Liverpool, of course, have their unique touches like the paddle tennis court constructed for intense staff battles, a special goalkeeping area and three newly-laid GrassMaster hybrid pitches.

Klopp did not just consider the features of the building, but the fundamentals too. The development squad will not have automatic access to designated first-team areas; they need to earn that right through application and attitude. He also wanted Liverpool to have a panoramic view when piecing together their plans, so captain Jordan Henderson and vice-captain James Milner were consulted about their thoughts.

Naturally, Edwards, Inglethorpe and Lijnders were also involved in designing the perfect new football HQ. On 9 September 2016, when 17 years of stadium false dawns was ended by Fenway Sports Group opening the £115 million redeveloped Main Stand, the owners were delighted Klopp was the man tasked with filling it with life by engaging the supporters. The success of that investment — not just in terms of matchday revenue (rising from £59 million to £84 million since 2015) and commercial opportunities but also enhancing the atmosphere and experience of the stadium — has led to plans to upgrade the Anfield Road stand.

That undertaking of around £60 million, increasing overall capacity to 61,000, was primarily advocated by Klopp and Gordon. A bigger, better Anfield is a platform for a more powerful Liverpool. More than ever, Klopp is determined to catapult the club to the next level.

'The longer you are somewhere, the more you feel a responsibility,' he admits. 'In this moment, we are the right coaches for this team, 100 per cent. And that means we don't stop, we don't get comfortable, we do more.

'We don't think about what we've done. It is a really exciting future with the new training ground, the young players coming through and the boys still hungry to create special times. When the club started the talks for the new contract, I couldn't imagine being anywhere else. It was speaking to the family and deciding how long, but there was not a doubt that I wanted to stay.'

Klopp's last extension, announced on 13 December 2019 and effective until 2024, was his third contract at Liverpool. It was universally celebrated but is it easy to forget that FSG were criticised for giving him a six-year deal in the summer of 2016, eight months after his appointment and following two lost finals.

'I found it strange,' former Liverpool midfielder Didi Hamann reacted. 'You don't get stability from a six-year contract — you get it from good work in the transfer market. He had an impact and has improved some players but if you look at the pure facts, the points average didn't improve dramatically from Brendan Rodgers' time. They have lost two finals — both they could or should have won — and then the club make a decision with their heart and not their head and extend the contract.'

That was not an alien opinion at the time. However, those within the club could see the unquantifiable impact Klopp was having. 'You can't really measure how he makes you feel as an individual and as a group,' Henderson says. John Achterberg adds that you can't put a price on what he's done at Liverpool. 'If you look at the money other clubs have spent to win compared to what we have, it tells you that you can't buy everything: not the atmosphere, not the team spirit, not a top working environment. You still have to create something special and the boss did that all through the club without needing to spend like crazy. That is not his way. And he sticks to what he believes in, which gives the club confidence.'

When principal owner John W Henry shared his response to an unprecedented season on Liverpool's channels in August 2020, he reserved an entire section to pay tribute to Klopp. 'Watching Jürgen get emotional made all of us emotional,' he said. 'I could go on and on about Jürgen and how his heart is larger than his frame, how his enthusiasm affects all of us positively every day. But I think what is important is he is determined every day to do the right thing, whether it's with regard to what happens on the pitch, whether it's regard to nutrition for the club. He is just determined every day to do the right thing and that rubs off. He works every day with Mike Gordon and Michael Edwards, two people that I've met that have the strongest moral code you could imagine. It's quite amazing to be involved with people on a day-to-day basis who are really talented and really committed to what they do.'

Henry has admitted 'the Premier League is the most difficult league in the world to win and the most difficult challenge that I have ever faced'. When Gordon told him about having the opportunity to meet Klopp in New York, it was the most excited he'd been as the club's owner, but not even he could have forecast this scale of achievement and the manager's diligence in improving every sphere of Liverpool.

Klopp was vacationing with his wife, Ulla, in Lisbon when his agent Marc Kosicke called him to set up the face-to-face interview with FSG in Manhattan. He had been set on a one-year sabbatical and promised his family he would stick to the break. But this . . . it felt right. 'We were on holiday in Lisbon and I got a call from my agent,' he said in the BBC documentary *The 30 Year Wait*. 'He told me about the interest of Liverpool. So our plans at that moment looked completely different actually, because we wanted to make more holidays! I told my family and my boys were immediately like "yes!" I looked in Ulla's eyes and she was "er, when?"

'When you make such a big promise like I did when

I left Dortmund, that we were going to have a year to ourselves, and after four months you come around the corner with different plans, you have to ask at least. I was pretty much on fire from the first second really, they didn't have to convince me.'

A year after Klopp's appointment, his work had commanded praise from an idol of his, but Liverpool's age-old enemy. 'He has done a really good job and revived Liverpool's enthusiasm,' former Manchester United manager Sir Alex Ferguson said in an interview with German magazine *Kicker*.

'It can happen that big clubs lose it. For two decades, Liverpool changed managers without building their own identity. You can now well and truly sense that you have to count them in this year. You can see Klopp's dedication on the sideline — I'm convinced his work in training is similar. He's a strong personality. That's absolutely vital at a big club. I'm worried about him because the one thing United don't want is Liverpool to get above us.'

Ferguson was rightly concerned and when Klopp was crowned the LMA Manager of the Year in July 2020, the Scot wanted to share his congratulations as a five-time winner of the award and as an admirer of the Reds tactician. 'You thoroughly deserved it, the performance level of your team was outstanding,' Fergie told broadcasters.

'Your personality runs right throughout the whole club. It was a marvellous performance. I'll forgive you for waking me up at 3.30 am to tell me you have won the league!'

A Liverpool manager calling Ferguson at that time with that news seemed like such fantasy given the last three decades. But Klopp was able to make the unlikely possible because he is so rooted in reality. He is not the champion of everything, he is just the man trying to be the champion of everything again.

Gordon and Edwards greatly appreciate Klopp's trait of not dwelling on the past, whether positive or not, and it's one they share. Talk of being champions of Europe, England and the world ended when the brief summer break ahead of 2020–21 was over. When players were asked about it during media commitments on pre-season, they automatically switched focus to what they need to achieve, not what was already done.

'The character of the leader informs the character of the team,' Pep Lijnders says. While Klopp admits it was 'absolutely overwhelming' to see all the trophies together which 'felt big and was so special for the people involved,' he makes it clear, 'I don't carry it around with me.

'How silly would it be to wake up in the morning and think "we are champions of England, Europe and the world" when all the other clubs don't sleep to catch us. What we did was good, but it's gone. We have to do the highest preparation again, keep the highest focus because we want to stay successful. We think constantly about how we do that. That is what is in my mind and nothing else.'

Klopp had been in Germany on holiday at the end of 2019–20 and while he appreciates how proud everyone is of the achievement and all the congratulations he received, he doesn't like the feeling of finality around that.

'The people are pretty proud and it's nice. We are proud as well, but it's only the start of something and not the end — I cannot see differently. We only started winning and that doesn't mean we will win from now on all the time, of course. But it means, of course we want to win again. And now we can say it, but we really have to show it. We don't get stuck on what happened before, we really have to go again with everything we have. One day, when we finish our careers, we can sit back and think of all the wonderful times. Now, we still work.'

When Klopp and Ulla left Germany for Liverpool, they were full of optimism but there was also apprehension. They had no idea how they would adjust to the city, to the unfamiliarity, to the demands and pressures of English football. They had been blessed with

Mainz and Dortmund, clubs that became their extended family during a 14-year period.

Could they possibly get that fortunate again? 'I didn't expect that we have so many friends after a pretty short period of time,' Klopp admits. 'And how can you expect that? So look, we had a really close relationship to the people in Dortmund and Mainz — we still have it, which is nice. But then you always think, "Okay, it cannot be like this everywhere." And it's true that it is not like this everywhere. But I am so lucky to find these clubs. I have found so many friends for life. And that also makes it difficult to think about leaving.

'It was an easy decision when Liverpool first called us. It was an easy decision for the six-year deal and it was an easy decision to stay until 2024. My family love it here, they love the club, they love the feeling they get from the people and so we were happy to make these choices together to stay. As a team, we have had problems. And we will have more problems. You have to deal with success. And if you're not successful, [you] have to be able to do everything to be successful. We enjoy the challenge and we are really on fire for it.

'We have a really good time even though we work at the highest intensity. Everybody wants to play their part in creating this kind of environment and it helps us. We are Liverpool and we really like and feel honour that we are Liverpool. We want to show it every day.

Who wants to leave Liverpool now? I can't imagine a good reason to. We have another four years and there's a lot we can still do. We want to use the time we have and we will.'

No one at Liverpool can contemplate the post-Klopp world. 'I don't want to think about that,' Henderson says. 'Right now, we're at our highest moment, but we have to maximise it and get all we can from it and that's on us. Whether you've won the Champions League or Premier League or lost those trophies, the mentality and desire has to absolutely be at 100 per cent. It can never be anything less and that's really something the gaffer has worked into us. There is so much he has given us.'

In 2008, Klopp told *Stern* magazine that life was 'about leaving better places behind. About not taking yourself too seriously. About giving your all. About loving and being loved.'

He has mastered that essence of life. When he leaves Liverpool, he will be missed. But Klopp's impact will linger, his legacy extending beyond silverware and full-throttle football — touching a club and its people so deeply, rejuvenating it and them so comprehensively.

Acknowledgments

The ability to document Liverpool's staggering transformation under Jürgen Klopp owes everything to so many people, not least the man himself. He has been incredibly generous with his time and thoughts, not just on football but on life over the past five years.

From Melwood to Hong Kong, and from California to New York and to Austria, he has sat down to exclusively share his methodology, always displaying honesty, warmth and humility.

Huge thanks to Liverpool captain Jordan Henderson, who is an absolute credit to the club. His willingness to go and above and beyond to help anyone he can, should be as iconic as his silverware shuffles.

Adam Lallana's kindness, care and contributions will never be forgotten. An overflow of gratitude goes to Pep Lijnders, John Achterberg, Mark Leyland and

Danielle McNally, not only for their assistance with the book but for their help over the years.

I'm thankful to the many brilliant minds who shared in-depth details off the record to help educate myself and the readers.

Matt McCann, when doors were closed on a young South African female trying to break into the industry here, you bucked the trend and respected my work enough to trust me with opportunities and access. There are countless people who talk about wanting to make a change in terms of diversifying the football landscape off the pitch, but you were actioning it long before it became a national talking point. I will be eternally grateful for all the help, career advice and gin! That extends to Joe Questier, James Carroll, Chris Shaw, Phil Reade and all the others at Liverpool – honestly too many of you to mention, you good eggs! – who took me in and offered friendship and family to a person so far away from home. TAW, I'm looking at you too.

To the Merseyside pack, cheers for setting the standards, the transcribing, the tips and for the camaraderie on our travels. Love to *Goal,* who gave me the platform to showcase my work, and every organisation since that brought me in, allowed me to shine and exposed me to gems like Alexis Nunes and Rob Dawson.

Special thanks to the *Independent,* the first publication to use my work in the UK and my amazing

ACKNOWLEDGMENTS

current employers. Ben Burrows, you are so appreciated for your understanding and accommodation as an editor. I am chuffed be part of such a brilliant team. Miguel, we'll always have the drama of Madrid!

Shoutouts to the hugely supportive Cody Duffy at Liverpool One Waterstones, to all the booksellers who have supported the book so enthusiastically, HarperCollins' Adam Murray for his plugging away, PR queen Alice Murphy-Pyle, and all the others working behind the scenes on the book. Tom Whiting channelled his inner Mo Salah and superbly sped through editing while still being surgical.

Jonathan de Peyer, you gave me the most ridiculous deadline going, but you also gave me the chance to do something I have longed to do for an age. You have no idea how much this means to me.

To every reader, listener and viewer who has supported my journey – to you, holding this book in your hand – you've assisted me with a perfectly weighted through ball.

To every individual who has helped shape me along the way and encouraged a girl to dream, to never lose light, you are special souls.

To the family and friends I had to leave back home in South Africa to pursue my passion, I carry you with me permanently. These are all your successes. I love you.

I seriously cannot thank you all enough.

Image captions

1. Liverpool's new German manager Jurgen Klopp poses with a shirt after a press conference announcing his appointment at Anfield on 9 October 2015. Klopp described his job as "the biggest challenge" in world football (Paul Ellis/AFP via Getty Images)
2. Klopp leads his players in saluting the crowd after drawing 2-2 in the Premier League against West Bromwich Albion at Anfield on 13 December 2015. (Oli Scarff/AFP via Getty Images)
3. Klopp and James Milner commiserate after Liverpool's defeat in the Europa League final against Sevilla at the St. Jakob-Park in Basel, 18 May 2016. They lost the game 3-1. (Imago sport-fotodienst via PA Images)
4. Klopp is thrown into the air as he celebrates with

his players and staff after winning the Champions League Final against Tottenham Hotspur at the Estadio Wanda Metropolitano in Madrid, 1 June 2019. Liverpool won 2-0 (Laurence Griffiths/ Getty Images)

5. Klopp and Henderson celebrate victory in the 2019 Champions League Final (Laurence Griffiths/ Getty Images)

6. Klopp with the trophy after winning the Champions League final (Matthias Hangst/Getty Images)

7. Fans line the streets of Liverpool for open-top bus parade on 2 June 2019 to celebrate their Champions League win. (Oli Scarff/AFP via Getty Images)

8. Liverpool's Sadio Mane celebrates scoring his side's third goal during the Premier League match between Liverpool FC and Manchester City at Anfield on 20 November 2019 (Alex Dodd - CameraSport via Getty Images)

9. Klopp signs a contract extension and chats with Sporting Director Michael Edwards and Mike Gordon, FSG President at Melwood Training Ground on 13 December 2019 (John Powell/ Liverpool FC via Getty Images)

10. Alisson Becker and Virgil van Dijk of Liverpool with the FIFA Club World Cup as Liverpool defeated CR Flamengo 1-0 at the Khalifa International Stadium in Doha, Qatar on 21

December 2019 (Andrew Powell/Liverpool FC via Getty Images)

11. Klopp, assistant managers Peter Krawietz and Pepijn Lijnders, goalkeeping coaches John Achterberg and Jack Robinson and development coach Vitor Matos with the FIFA Club World Cup (Andrew Powell/Liverpool FC via Getty Images)

12. Midfielder James Milner celebrates with teammates after scoring their second goal from the penalty spot during the Premier League match against Leicester City at the King Power Stadium in Leicester, 26 December 2019 (Oli Scarff/AFP via Getty Images)

13. Mohamed Salah celebrates a goal to make it 2-0 against Manchester United at Anfield in the Premier League on 19 January 2020 (Michael Regan/Getty Images)

14. Roberto Firmino scores his side's second goal of the game against Wolverhampton Wanderers at Molineux on 23 January 2020 (David Davies/ EMPICS Sport via PA Images)

15. Captain Henderson lifts the Premier League trophy at Anfield on 22 July 2020. (Photo by Phil Noble/ Pool/AFP via Getty Images